# Vocabulary for the TOEIC® test

Serena Murdoch-Stern
David Mayer

ISBN : 978-2-09-810924-7

# Avant propos

Il n'est pas nécessaire d'avoir une connaissance approfondie du vocabulaire du monde des affaires pour réussir le TOEIC. Cependant, l'étendue des sujets abordés dans le TOEIC impose une bonne connaissance des termes d'anglais général et des affaires pour comprendre rapidement, ne pas perdre de temps et obtenir un bon résultat à l'examen. Produire un « bon anglais » est aujourd'hui essentiel dans le monde du travail : votre vocabulaire professionnel ou universitaire vous aidera à améliorer votre score au TOEIC, et la révision du TOEIC boostera votre carrière !!

Le livret est organisé de façon à s'y retrouver facilement. Si vous avez peu de temps, travaillez vos points faibles d'abord, puis les sujets plus généraux tels que voyager, sortir... C'est la raison pour laquelle les sujets que vous connaissez probablement le moins se trouvent au début et non à la fin du livret ! Les exercices sont très variés – lorsque vous êtes fatigués, privilégiez ceux qui sont courts et faciles. Et le matin, de bonne heure, entreprenez ceux qui vous posent plus de difficulté !

Partout dans le livre vous trouverez des petits exercices sur les homonymes, les mots qui prêtent à confusion, et d'autres jeux de vocabulaire. L'objectif est de stimuler votre appétit – pour que vous ayez envie d'aller plus loin et d'apprendre encore plus de vocabulaire ! Établissez une liste des mots que vous ne connaissez pas, pour la revoir de temps en temps. Il faut apprendre un nouveau mot au moins 3 fois avant de bien le mémoriser.

Essayez de travailler sans dictionnaire au début. Si vous n'y arrivez pas, vous pouvez en utiliser un, mais évitez les traducteurs automatiques : vous ferez moins fonctionner votre mémoire et c'est beaucoup moins efficace. Dans la section réponse, vous trouverez également des synonymes et des « traductions » de l'anglais américain / britannique.

Lorsque vous faites des exercices sur des textes longs, essayez de lire d'abord les questions, puis lisez une première fois le texte rapidement. Ensuite, prenez le temps de faire l'exercice tranquillement. Vous devrez travailler de cette façon à l'examen, donc autant vous entraîner tout de suite.

Nous ne pouvons pas vous garantir que vous trouverez ici tous les mots que vous rencontrerez à l'examen, donc n'oubliez pas de lire des livres, des magazines, et des journaux en anglais (commencez par des textes courts, puis soyez plus ambitieux). Plus vous lirez, plus vous comprendrez vite. Vous pouvez également regarder la télévision et des films ou « soap operas » en anglais, et bénéficier de la richesse des sites Internet anglophones. En un rien de temps, vous utiliserez l'anglais comme votre langue maternelle !

## *The Company* 6



## *The Administrative Departments* 18



## *The Product* 40

## *Assorted Business Activities* 56



## *Communicating* 72



## *Travelling & Entertainment* 88



## *Answers Section* 115

# 1 Types of Business

## A. WHAT KIND OF BUSINESS?

*Match the question to the answer.*

**Answers:**

**1.** The corporate sector •

**2.** Manufacturer •

**3.** Import / export company •

**4.** The heavy manufacturing sector such as automobiles, chemicals, steel, paper, etc. •

**5.** Cottage industry •

**6.** Small and middle-sized companies •

**7.** Public Limited Company •

**8.** Least Developed Countries •

**9.** Mail-order company •

**10.** Craftsman •

**11.** Primary (extraction or harvesting raw materials), secondary (manufactures finished goods), tertiary (or service sector), quaternary (intellectual activities) and quinary (high-level decision making) •

**12.** Make sure it's Limited Liability. •

**Questions:**

• **a)** What does SMC stand for?

• **b)** What are the five different sectors of the economy?

• **c)** What is a company which sells or purchases goods abroad?

• **d)** What's the name of a company where you order goods through the post?

• **e)** What do you call someone who makes goods by industrial means?

• **f)** What is a small-scale industry, often run from home on a family basis?

• **g)** The name for a workman skilled in a trade (stonemason, miller, potter...)

• **h)** What does LDC stand for?

• **i)** How about PLC?

• **j)** What on earth is a "smokestack industry"?

• **k)** If the personal sector relates to households, what is the name for the sector related to firms?

• **l)** How can I be sure not to lose more money than the capital I invest in a firm?

## B. WHICH BUSINESS SECTOR?

*Can you find the following 27 business sectors in the word puzzle (up, down, across, on more than one line...)? Note: (industry) and (work) are not in the puzzle.*

- Electronics and IT services
- Aerospace, Marine & Defence
- Automotive (industry)
- Banking and Financial services
- Sustainable Development
- Pharmaceutical and Healthcare
- Materials and Engineering
- Environmental industries
- Construction (industry)
- Charity (work)
- Telecommunications
- Textile (industry)
- Transport
- Tourism
- Packing plant
- Retail
- Mining (industry)
- Logistics platform
- Metallurgy
- Biotechnology
- Publishing
- Avionics
- Chemicals
- Broadcasting
- Manufacturing
- Agriculture
- Fashion
- Leisure (industry)

| | | | | | | | | | | | | | | | | | | | | | | | | | | | | | |
|---|---|---|---|---|---|---|---|---|---|---|---|---|---|---|---|---|---|---|---|---|---|---|---|---|---|---|---|---|---|
| D | R | T | D | M | C | H | L | T | E | X | T | I | L | E | Q | I | P | K | H | T | F | D | E | H | J | K | L | L | A |
| C | H | E | M | I | C | A | L | S | H | H | E | N | X | H | K | T | E | E | J | K | C | E | J | B | D | L | M | T | E |
| Q | H | L | R | N | F | F | J | F | R | K | F | D | S | R | P | A | C | K | I | N | G | P | L | A | N | T | D | G | R |
| D | F | E | F | I | J | R | U | U | L | G | S | U | F | J | S | D | J | K | R | J | Y | I | L | N | D | F | D | R | O |
| D | G | C | D | N | J | L | T | E | G | H | R | S | S | A | U | T | O | M | O | T | I | V | E | K | F | J | R | S | S |
| P | S | T | F | G | E | I | R | D | H | E | D | T | L | Q | S | J | L | R | S | J | Y | J | D | I | D | E | G | U | P |
| U | D | R | F | R | F | J | A | D | J | R | G | R | O | R | T | D | J | R | F | U | J | F | R | N | D | R | F | R | A |
| B | I | O | T | E | C | H | N | O | L | O | G | Y | G | D | A | M | E | T | A | L | L | U | R | G | Y | J | D | S | C |
| L | D | N | F | D | R | H | S | R | J | K | I | V | I | F | I | R | U | K | F | D | G | K | L | & | F | R | J | U | E |
| I | F | I | D | R | F | H | P | J | L | M | T | D | S | R | N | F | R | H | J | U | K | K | L | F | R | G | T | D | M |
| S | F | C | R | H | R | F | O | H | K | L | F | D | T | M | A | N | U | F | A | C | T | U | R | I | N | G | F | D | A |
| H | S | S | F | R | D | G | R | D | G | J | K | L | I | D | B | R | J | K | I | L | G | R | J | N | D | R | A | H | R |
| I | F | & | D | R | H | J | T | R | H | J | K | K | C | R | L | D | H | J | K | L | I | L | N | A | F | J | G | K | I |
| N | D | I | R | H | M | A | T | E | R | I | A | L | S | & | E | N | G | I | N | E | E | R | I | N | G | D | R | R | N |
| G | D | T | F | R | H | K | L | U | K | L | V | T | P | F | D | R | J | L | F | R | H | J | I | C | R | J | I | D | E |
| D | F | S | K | M | I | T | R | E | Z | D | F | G | L | S | E | D | S | Z | H | T | K | Q | D | I | E | Z | C | D | & |
| D | S | E | J | J | K | R | Z | S | E | K | L | U | A | Q | V | S | E | G | E | G | H | R | H | A | D | E | U | Q | D |
| S | H | R | D | E | T | U | K | I | R | D | F | E | T | A | E | A | D | E | B | A | H | J | Y | L | A | E | L | A | E |
| E | N | V | I | R | O | N | M | E | N | T | A | L | F | E | L | E | H | J | R | A | H | J | I | S | E | Z | T | Z | F |
| D | S | I | N | D | U | S | T | R | I | E | S | E | O | D | O | J | K | L | O | E | H | J | L | E | I | S | U | R | E |
| S | E | C | H | A | R | I | T | Y | N | R | H | E | R | F | P | A | H | P | A | D | C | W | E | R | E | D | K | E | N |
| O | P | E | E | G | I | E | A | A | K | L | I | M | M | E | M | T | E | I | D | O | J | L | E | V | R | E | E | C | C |
| D | E | S | P | L | S | Z | V | S | Q | V | O | J | E | R | E | S | L | N | C | V | U | R | Z | I | D | L | D | I | E |
| A | D | K | R | E | M | I | I | M | L | O | N | E | P | C | N | D | E | J | A | K | O | P | E | C | R | D | F | Z | M |
| S | V | T | E | L | E | C | O | M | M | U | N | I | C | A | T | I | O | N | S | D | E | R | N | E | O | P | Y | E | R |
| D | N | L | T | O | R | S | N | A | Q | Y | J | O | P | M | B | E | R | C | T | D | J | O | L | S | A | N | L | R | P |
| D | G | J | A | A | T | Y | I | U | I | C | C | P | E | L | L | E | N | B | I | T | I | O | P | D | C | Y | J | P | N |
| A | H | K | I | J | P | L | C | O | N | S | T | R | U | C | T | I | O | N | N | A | J | L | F | F | M | O | I | E | R |
| B | D | E | L | A | J | L | S | Q | E | N | O | P | E | R | X | E | H | L | G | A | D | I | L | R | Z | C | C | V | H |
| P | H | A | R | M | A | C | E | U | T | I | C | A | L | & | H | E | A | L | T | H | C | A | R | E | A | J | L | D | S |

## 2 Company Structure

### A MULTINATIONAL COMPANY

↘ *Put the following words into the right place in the diagram.*

- Overseas branch
- B.U. Business Unit (SBU Strategic Business Unit) / Division
- Shareholder
- Department
- Parent Company
- Partnership
- Head office
- Subsidiary
- Sister Company
- Turnover

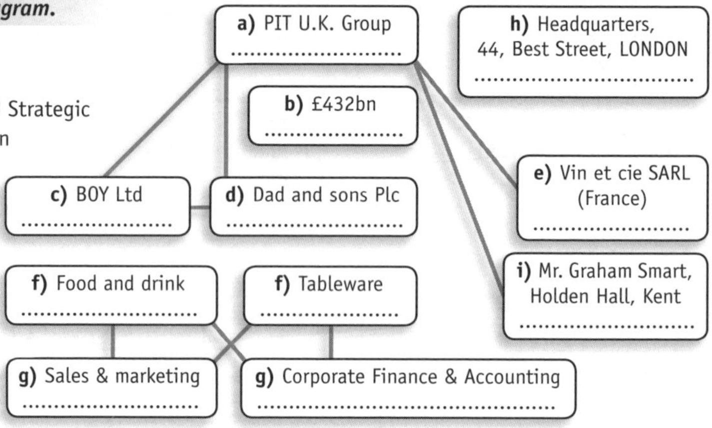


## 3 Company History

### A. BUSINESS IS BOOMING

↘ *Put the words into the right place in the story. Don't forget to put the verb into the right tense. Look carefully at the number of words you need.*

- Establish / set up
- Takeover
- Partnership
- Location
- Buyout
- Share capital
- Founder
- Market share
- Premises
- Ranks / ranking
- Merger
- Turnover
- Based in …
- Core business
- Company policy
- Growth
- Competitors
- Forward planning
- Company image
- Go public
- In-company / in-house
- Incorporate
- Joint management
- Memorandum and articles of association

Welcome to Workers & Wellness Gmbh. The **(1)** F__________, Mrs Sarah Smiley, **(2)** S__________ U__ the company, which is **(3)** B__________ I___ Phoenix, Arizona, in 1909. The company's **(4)** C__________ B__________ (or principal activity) is an advisory service to improve the conditions of

operatives in the workplace. Clever **(5)** F__________ P__________ and precise forecasting all along has enabled this family company to become a serious competitor on the global market.
Firstly, to **(6)** I__________ the company, the **(7)** M__________ _____ A__________ __ A__________ were drawn up. The **(8)** L__________ was chosen in a Greenfield site just outside Phoenix, and ground-breaking worker-friendly **(9)** P__________ were built, including sports facilities, rest rooms and a gourmet restaurant. An **(10)** I___-H__________ promotion policy has encouraged staff loyalty, a key factor in the success of the **(11)** M__________ with the Happiness Hotel chain in 1954.
**(12)** The considerable G__________ of Workers & Wellness has been exemplary. Having started with a **(13)** S__________ C__________ of $5,000, the **(14)** T__________ in 2008 was over $258,000, an amazing sum. Despite hot competition in their market sector, Workers and Wellness's **(15)** C__________ have never been able to match their efficiency and responsiveness. The company now **(16)** R__________ 1st in the corporate rankings in their field, and have a 63% **(17)** M__________ S__________, a very high percentage of the market segment.
The first important development was the **(18)** P__________ created with Health & Wealth in 1923. The **(19)** J__________ M__________ of the two companies, working well alongside each other, led to further investments and growth. The **(20)** T__________ (friendly of course!) of Feel Good in 1966, in which Workers & Wellness bought 98% of the stock, was closely followed by the purchase of a controlling interest, or **(21)** B__________, of Relax Max Inc. in 1975. The company decided to **(22)** G_____ P__________ (or offer their stock to the public rather than keeping to private shareholders) to raise more capital in 1983 and is now listed on the stock exchange index.
**(23)** C __________ P__________ has always been the same – set an example. If the staff at Workers & Wellness were contented, then they should be able to spread the word. **(24)** C__________ I__________ is also very important. Everyone who works for the company is expected to dress in corporate colours (blue and white), which can vary from jeans to a smart suit. Just take one look at all their smiley faces, it's no wonder this corporation has gone from strength to strength over a century.

## B. 6 HORRIBLE HOMONYMS

*Choose the right answer.*

**1. Affect / effect**
**a)** The new competitor might .......... our sales. **b)** His speech had a great ......... on the sales team.
**2. Build / Billed**
**a)** Have you ............... the customer yet? **b)** Did you ............... that house alone?
**3. Cell / sell**
**a)** I ............... phones. **b)** His ............... phone.
**4. Cent / scent / sent**
**a)** I wouldn't give a ........ for that. **b)** Has he ......... the parcel off? **c)** That's the most lovely ........
**5. Complement / compliment**
**a)** The accessories are a ........... to the equipment. **b)** The boss said I was efficient. What a ............!
**6. Council / counsel**
**a)** The local ........... had the old factory demolished. **b)** Take .......... before you decide to sue.

## C. THE RISE AND FALL OF THE COMPANY

*Find a synonym in the lists to the word(s) underlined in the sentence.*

**ORGANISATIONAL CHANGES**

Cutbacks - Build up - Tighten up – Streamline – Restructure – Downsize – Update – Upgrade - Phase in - Strengthen

**1.** We have to reorganize how we work things. ....................
**2.** We also have to make reductions in our overheads. ....................
**3.** An improvement to our I.T. system wouldn't go amiss. ....................
**4.** The subsidiary in Austria needs to be made smaller. ....................
**5.** We have to bring in slowly the new product to keep production up to full capacity. ....................
**6.** We should develop better customer relations. ....................
**7.** Production could be made smoother and less time would be wasted. ....................
**8.** The new methods manager has certainly made stronger the department. ....................
**9.** Gentlemen, to increase our margins you will have to economise on your expenses. ....................
**10.** So, could you bring us up to date on the latest developments? ....................

**DOWNHILL**

Steady decrease - Downward trend – Weakening - Sharp fall

**11.** Our company indicators this business year show a worrying descending tendency. ....................
**12.** In January there was a sudden drop in inter-company sales. ....................
**13.** The regular decline of customers is a headache for the marketing department. ....................
**14.** Our diminishing position in the market is just one sign of the bad results for 2008. ..................

**CORPORATE TURNAROUND**

General improvement - Move forward - Marked progress - Constant rise - Upward trend - Dramatic increase

**15.** There has been continuous improvement in our sales over the past 5 years. ....................
**16.** The most impressive growth rate was a 35% increase in 2007, a record year. ....................
**17.** Overall progress has been made in administration. ....................
**18.** However, a noticeable advancement has been made in production streamlining. ....................
**19.** The results show that the company is on a tendency towards the top. ....................
**20.** We need to advance from our current situation – let's set up a website. ....................

## A. ARE YOU AN ODD-JOB MAN?

↘ *Complete the six little crosswords. (The (2) indicates the number of words.)*

**a. Healthcare and welfare**

**Across: 1.** A medical specialist who operates to treat injury, etc. **2.** Someone who uses exercises, massages, etc. for treatment **3.** A person licensed to practise medicine. For example, a G.P.

**Down: 4.** Agents who help individuals, groups or communities (2) **5.** A medical caretaker, often in a hospital **6.** Someone trained in pharmacy, a druggist

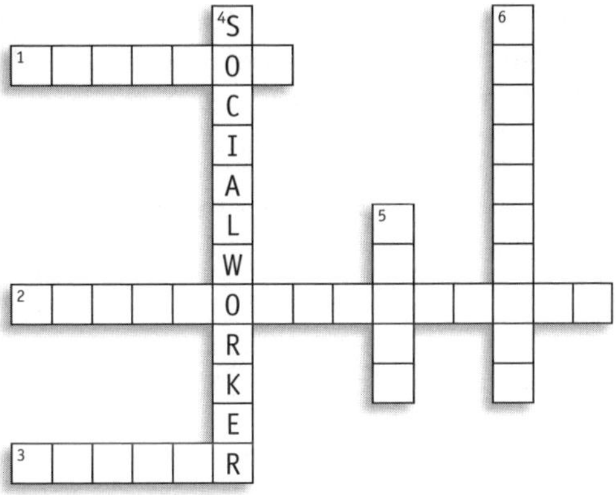

**b. Finance & legal**

**Across: 1.** An employee of a bank or company who analyses financial results (2) **2.** Someone who keeps and inspects financial accounts **3.** Someone who records the transactions and accounts of a business (2)

**Down: 4.** Someone appointed to audit or examine accounts **5.** A person who hears and determines cases in court **6.** A person who practises law (General term to cover all) **7.** A person in charge of funds or revenues

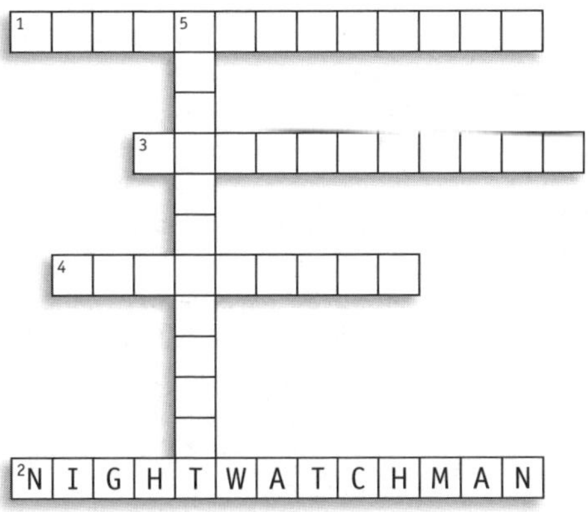


**c. Security and public services**

**Across: 1.** Someone who enforces the law (2)
**2.** Someone who keeps guard at night (2) **3.** A person who fights fires for the fire dept. (2) **4.** A person employed to look after a building or person

**Down: 5.** A public official or government employee (2)

→

### d. Craftsmen & the outdoor world

**Across: 1.** A specialist in the development of renewable energy (3) **2.** Someone who cultivates a farm **3.** A person who makes things out of wood **4.** A person who builds or repairs buildings

**Down: 5.** Someone who installs and maintains wiring systems **6.** A person who installs and repairs pipes and plumbing

### e. Education, the written word, the arts, the media

**Across: 1.** Someone who changes words from one language to another **2.** A private tutor in sport or business **3.** Someone who writes books **4.** Someone who takes photographs professionally **5.** A person who is skilled in music **6.** A performer who sings **7.** Someone who looks after a library

**Down: 8.** Person employed to report news **9.** Someone who teaches **10.** Someone who acts **11.** Someone who designs buildings

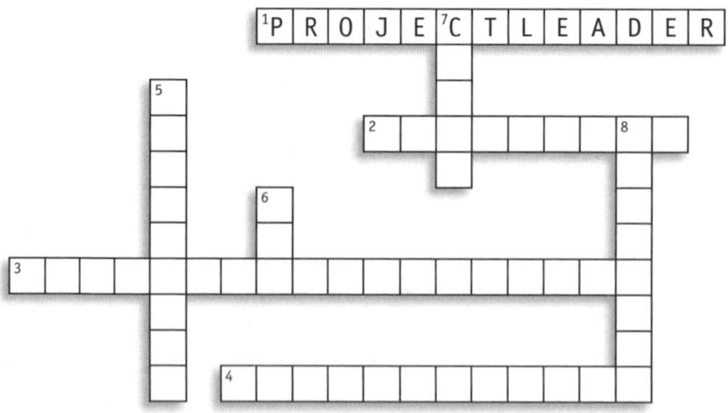


### f. In a factory

**Across: 1.** The person who heads a project (2) **2.** The person responsible for buying things **3.** A sales representative who sells at residences (4) **4.** A person who produces goods on a large scale with machines

**Down: 5.** Someone who works a machine on the factory floor **6.** Public Relations Officer (Acronym) **7.** An employee who does written work in an office **8.** A person who does engineering

## B. AN ORGANISATION CHART

*The American titles are given in this exercise. British English equivalents, if available and, other options can be found in the answers section. Put the people into the right circle on the chart.*

**a)** Domestic Sales Manager
**b)** Purchaser
**c)** Chairman and C.E.O.
**d)** EH&S Manager
**e)** Senior Vice President (Corp Development)
**f)** Strategic Partner Marketing
**g)** R&D Director
**h)** General Manager
**i)** Quality Manager
**j)** Assembly Foreman
**k)** Chief Accountant
**g)** Vice President Human Resources
**h)** Chief Information Officer (C.I.O.)
**i)** Workshop Manager
**j)** Strategic Partner Sales
**k)** Chief Financial Officer (C.F.O.)
**l)** Production Director
**m)** Export Sales Manager
**n)** Vice President (Product Management)
**o)** Vice President (Sales and Business Development)
**p)** Senior Vice President (Manufacturing)

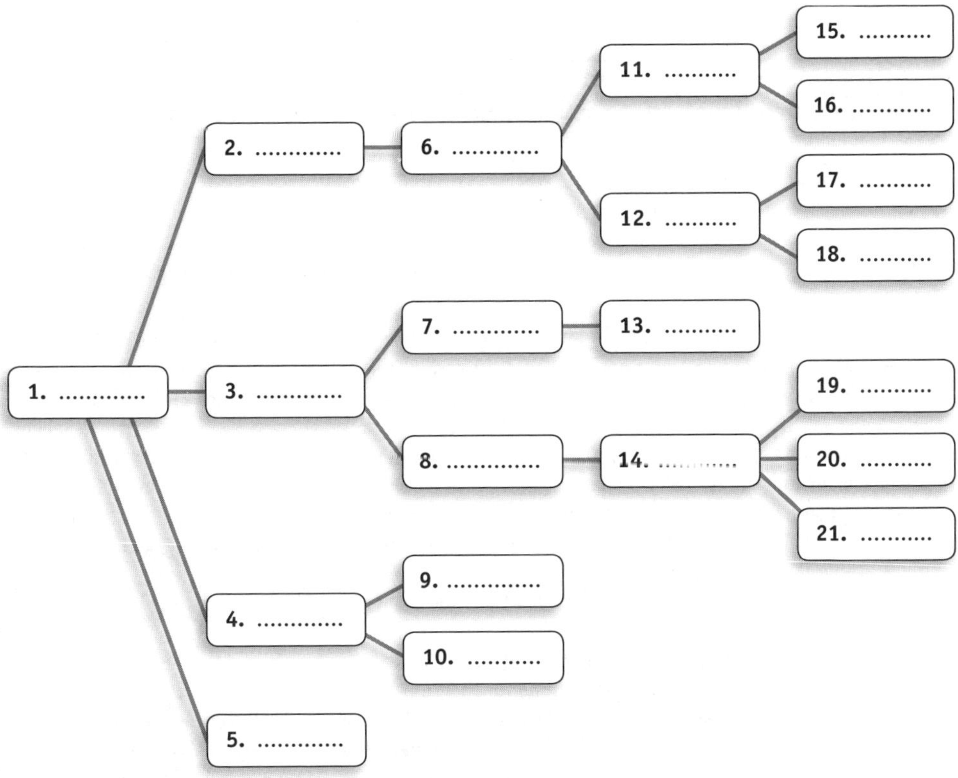

## C. WHO REPORTS TO WHOM?

↘ *Using the organisational chart above, fill in the following sentences.*

**is accountable to – in charge of – assists – reports to – responsible to – assisted by – responsible for – oversees**

**1.** The R&D Director is ___ ______________ __ Purchasing, Quality and EH&S.
**2.** The Vice President for Human Resources ______________ __ the C.F.O.
**3.** The Workshop Manager ___ ______________ __ the Production Director.
**4.** The Export Sales Manager ______________ the Strategic Partner for Sales.
**5.** The Assembly Foreman ______________ all the assembly lines.
**6.** The Chief Accountant is ______________ __ a bookkeeper.
**7.** The C.I.O. is ______________ __ the C.E.O.
**8.** The C.E.O. _____________________ the whole company!

## D. YOUR POSITION IN THE COMPANY

↘ *Look at the presentation, and replace the words in brackets by one of the words hereunder.*

**a)** Seasonal worker
**b)** Head
**c)** Temporary worker
**d)** Skilled worker
**e)** Colleague
**f)** Senior executive
**g)** Moonlighter
**h)** Guest worker
**i)** Apprentice
**j)** Out worker
**k)** Junior executive
**l)** Unskilled worker
**m)** Self-employed
**n)** Trainee
**o)** Casual worker
**p)** Supervisor

Welcome to our company. I would like to introduce you to some of the staff. Let's start in the offices, and then we'll move on to the factory floor. First of all, this is Peter, he's Head of Research, one of our **(1)** (upper grade managers) ........................... ; he is assisted by John, who is a **(2)** (lower grade manager) ........................... . Here is another of our **(3)** (co-workers) ..........................., Rachel, who is **(4)** (at the top of) ........................... the Finance Department. As we go past the I.T. (Information Technology) area, you'll probably see Sally, who looks after all our computers and information systems. She doesn't directly work for us but is **(5)** (works for herself) ..........................., and highly efficient! With her is her young **(6)** (someone being trained in a vocational area) ..........................., who is learning fast.
Now, let's move on to the workshops. First of all, I'd like you to meet our **(7)** (overseer) ......................, Michael, who manages everyone here.
Bob is a **(8)** (someone who has had training for his job) ..........................., and his workmate is Jo, who is an **(9)** (someone who has had no training for their job) ..........................., but who hopes to get some training in the near future on the assembly line. Manpower in the factor also includes a lot of people who come when we need more manpower, when we have to call on **(10)** (a short-term temporary labourer who is entitled to leave and other benefits) ........................... . In the summer, when we

have to make an awful lot of ice-cream tubs, we employ **(11)** (people who only work in a specific season) ............................ . We even have some **(12)** (people who make parts away from the premises) ............................, especially women so they can stay at home.
Yuri is **(13)** (a temporary worker from a foreign country) ............................; he'll be taking back all his experience to Israel at the end of the month. He looks very tired, I rather fear he's a **(14)** (someone who works at another job, often at night) ............................, and doing too much!
We also sometimes use **(15)** (a short-term temporary labourer who is not entitled to leave or other benefits) ............................ .
This is the youngest member of our team, Henry, who is an **(16)** (someone being trained in a skilled trade) ............................, and will be learning on-site for four years.
Now, let's go and get you settled into your office...

## 5 The Working Day

### A MULTINATIONAL COMPANY

↘ ***Match a word from column A to column B to find the solution to the clue.***

**TIME OFF**

| | | |
|---|---|---|
| **1.** Public • | • **A.** Leave | A legal holiday limiting work or business |
| **2.** Maternity • | • **B.** Off | Time off when you are expecting and just after having a baby |
| **3.** Sick • | • **C.** Holiday | Time off when you are unwell |
| **4.** Day • | • **D.** Leave | A working day when you do not go to work |
| **5.** Paid • | • **E.** Holiday | Holiday entitlement |

**WORKING HOURS**

| | | |
|---|---|---|
| **1.** Clock • | • **A.** Time | Register arrival at work on automatic time recorder |
| **2.** Knock • | • **B.** Out | Informal for to stop working |
| **3.** Full • | • **C.** In | Employed for a standard number of hours' working time |
| **4.** Office • | • **D.** Time | The hours between which the office is open |
| **5.** Flexi • | • **E.** Day | Flexible working hours at the beginning or end of the day |
| **6.** Part • | • **F.** A break | Employed for less than the standard number of hours' working time |
| **7.** Clock • | • **G.** Hours | Register time leaving work on automatic time recorder |
| **8.** Time • | • **H.** Off | An automatic time recorder |
| **9.** Take • | • **I.** Time | Stop working for a rest |
| **10.** Work • | • **J.** Clock | A day on which work can be done (sometimes not a Sunday) |

**WE ARE VERY BUSY**

| | | |
|---|---|---|
| **1.** 24/ • | • **A.** Shift | We work 24 hours a day, seven days a week. |
| **2.** Over • | • **B.** Hours | Hours worked in addition to the regular quantity of working hours |
| **3.** Night • | • **C.** Time | Working at night, from 9pm to 5am for example |
| **4.** Unsocial • | • **D.** 7 | Working outside the socially recognised working day |

## 6 On the Premises

### A. OPTIMISING PLANT LAYOUT

↘ *Put the different departments into the right place in the factory.*

**a)** Rest area, **b)** Car park **c)** Assembly line **d)** Delivery area (Receiving) **e)** Meeting room **f)** Workshops **g)** Quality control **h)** Packaging and warehousings **i)** Toilets **j)** Reception **k)** Caretaker's lodge **l)** Dispatch / Shipping **m)** Production line **n)** Sick room **o)** Staff canteen **p)** Administration offices

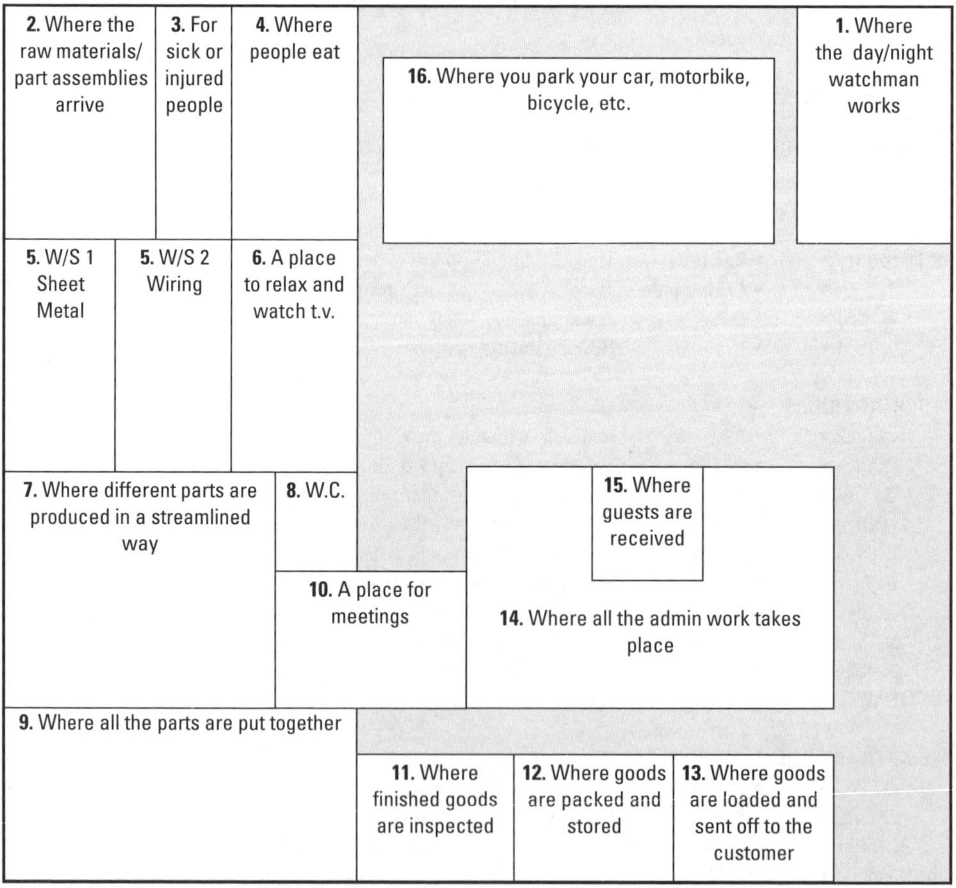

## B. COULD YOU TIDY UP YOUR OFFICE?!

↘ *Match the object to the number on the picture.*

**a)** Desktop computer
**b)** Bulletin board
**c)** Stapler
**d)** Pen
**e)** Drawer
**f)** Shredder
**g)** Desk
**h)** Ruler
**i)** Paper
**j)** Chair
**k)** Cell phone
**l)** File
**m)** Calendar
**n)** USB flash drive
**o)** Laptop computer
**p)** Rubber
**q)** Palmtop organiser
**r)** Calculator
**s)** Pencil
**t)** Waste bin

# 1 Finance

## A. ARE YOU GOOD AT NUMBERS?

*Match the number to the words.*

### 1. Counting

| | |
|---|---|
| **1.** 342 • | • **A.** A hundred |
| **2.** 1,000,000,000 • | • **B.** Three hundred (and) forty-two |
| **3.** 100 • | • **C.** One thousand four hundred (and) ninety-five |
| **4.** 100,000 • | • **D.** A hundred thousand |
| **5.** 1,495 • | • **E.** A million |
| **6.** 1,000,000 • | • **F.** A billion |

### 2. Confusion

| | |
|---|---|
| **1.** Nineteen fifty-five / oh seven fifty-five / five to eight pm • | • **A.** 1957 |
| **2.** Nought point oh one nine • | • **B.** $ 19.57 |
| **3.** Nineteen dollars and fifty-seven cents / Nineteen dollars fifty-seven • | • **C.** 19.55 / 07.55 / 7:55 in the evening |
| **4.** Nineteen thousand five hundred and seventy • | • **D.** 19.570 |
| **5.** Nineteen point five seven oh • | • **E.** 19,570 |
| **6.** Nineteen fifty-seven (year) • | • **F.** 0.019 |

### 3. Statistics

| | |
|---|---|
| **1.** 33.3% • | • **A.** Three by four by five metres |
| **2.** 3 x 4 x 5 m • | • **B.** One in twenty |
| **3.** 12 $m^2$ • | • **C.** Twelve cubic metres / metres cubed |
| **4.** 1:20 • | • **D.** Half a litre |
| **5.** 12 $m^3$ • | • **E.** Twelve square metres / metres squared |
| **6.** ½ l • | • **F.** Thirty-three point three percent |

### 4. Fractions

| | |
|---|---|
| **1.** Two-thirds • | • **A.** $^1/_4$ |
| **2.** Three-tenths • | • **B.** $^1/_2$ |
| **3.** Three-fourths / Three-quarters • | • **C.** $^3/_4$ |
| **4.** One-fourth / a quarter • | • **D.** $^2/_3$ |
| **5.** A half • | • **E.** $^5/_8$ |
| **6.** Five-eighths • | • **F.** $^3/_{10}$ |

**5. Maths**

| | |
|---|---|
| **1.** + • | • **A.** Minus / take away |
| **2.** - • | • **B.** Divided by |
| **3.** / • | • **C.** Three point three recurring |
| **4.** x • | • **D.** Times / multiplied by |
| **5.** 14 + 5 = 19 • | • **E.** Plus / and |
| **6.** 3.33333 or 5.66666 • | • **F.** Fourteen plus five equals nineteen |

***If you can't do any of these, you need to revise your numbers!***

Synonyms: Approximately £50 = Roughly £50 = About £50

## B. DIFFERENT KINDS OF ACCOUNTING

↘ ***Read the short texts, and decide which kind of accounting they refer to.***

**a)** Bookkeeping
**b)** Tax Accounting
**c)** Managerial Accounting
**d)** Auditing
**e)** Cost Accounting
**f)** "Creative" Accounting

**1.** Part of management accounting, to establish the cost of producing an item..............................
**2.** An independent and objective inspection of final accounts. .................................................
**3.** Questionable accounting methods to give an overstated net result. .........................................
**4.** Accounting used for planning, control and decision making. ..................................................
**5.** The methodical recording of business transactions.................................................................
**6.** Accounting which is focused on tax issues. ...........................................................................

## C. IN THE ACCOUNTS DEPARTMENT

↘ ***Find the word in the text which means:***

**1.** Reimburse ..........................................................................................................
**2.** Transfer an item to another item / date / account ....................................................
**3.** A fixed rate for car expenses ................................................................................
**4.** Be able to pay for .............................................................................................
**5.** Make a mistake when counting ..............................................................................
**6.** Travel and entertainment expenses charged to the company .....................................
**7.** An item in a written record ..................................................................................
**8.** A bill which has not been paid ..............................................................................
**9.** I owe you (promise to pay a debt) .........................................................................
**10.** A book to record monetary transactions ................................................................
**11.** Not budgeted or specified expenses ......................................................................
**12.** To give financial assistance or support ..................................................................→

→ Accountant: I'm sorry Bob; we really cannot afford to keep up with your expense account. Every time you put in your expenses the figures just don't add up, for example, travel expenses. The company has a standard mileage rate, but we cannot run to the fuel consumption of a vintage jaguar! And look here, what is this I.O.U. for a restaurant bill you have never paid?! We really cannot subsidize such a glamorous lifestyle any longer. I think you will have to make a gesture and pay back some of these amounts; I really cannot ask the clerk to make an entry in the ledger.
Bob: Maybe there has been a miscount, I'm sure that I haven't spent that much this year.
Accountant: Well, I can ask the bookkeeper to record some of the cocktails as incidental expenses, and hope that no one higher up will notice. But what do you want me to do about this unpaid invoice?
Bob: Pay it I suppose!! Maybe you could carry forward some of the expenses to next month; that would be less obvious.
Accountant: O.K. I'm giving you one last chance, and then...

## D. INVOICING AND PAYMENT

↘ ***Put the following words into the right balloon.***

• Payment past due • Overdue payment • Invoice • Subtotal • Mid-July • Owe • Hire • Purchase • Payment date • Prepaid • Bill for services rendered • Payment by instalments • Balance due / due date

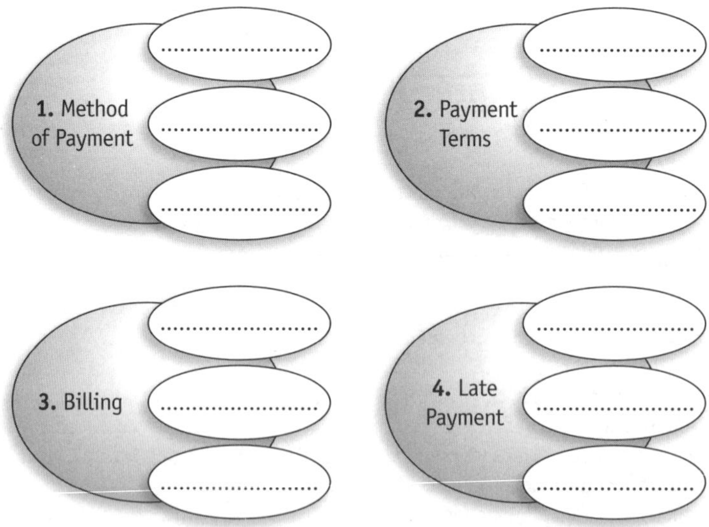

## E. FINANCIAL STATEMENTS

***Put a word from the list into the right place in the following 3 financial statements. Words can be used more than once, for example, Assets = 6 times, Revenue = twice.***

- Balance Sheet (1)
- Income Statement (1)
- Operating Expenses (2)
- Assets (6)
- Net Income (1)
- Revenue (2)
- Cash Flow Statement (1)
- Liabilities (6)

| | |
|---|---|
| **CREATIVE COMPANY**<br>**(1)** _______________<br>at 31st January 20.... *Or a Snapshot of a company's financial situation on a particular date* | $'000,000 |
| **Tangible & Intangible (2)** ____________ | |
| ***CURRENT (2)*** ________________ | |
| Cash & Cash Equivalents | 1,612 |
| Short Term Investments | 199 |
| Receivables | 1,234 |
| Inventories | 1,001 |
| Prepaid Expenses and Other | 1,504 |
| **TOTAL CURRENT (2)** _____________ | **5,550** |
| ***LONG TERM (2)*** ________________ | |
| Long Term Investments | 7,411 |
| Property, Plant & Equipment | 3,902 |
| Intangible Assets, Goodwill & I.P. | 1,800 |
| Accumulated Depreciation (or Amortisation) | N/A |
| Other Assets | N/A |
| **TOTAL (2)** ___________________ | **18,663** |
| **(3)** __________________________ | |
| ***CURRENT (3)*** __________________ | |
| Accounts Payable | 4,211 |
| Short Term Debt | 3,009 |
| Other Current (3) _________________ | N/A |
| **TOTAL CURRENT (3)** _____________ | **7,220** |
| **LONG TERM (3)** _________________ | |
| Long Term Debt | 721 |
| Other Liabilities (including Provision for Bad Debts) | 934 |
| **TOTAL (3)** _____________________ | **8,875** |
| **TOTAL STOCKHOLDER EQUITY** | **9,788** |
| **NET (2)**______________________ | **7,988** |

→

| (4) ____________ | Year ended 31st March 20-- |
|---|---|
| (5) ____________ | |
| Commission earned | |
| Sales | |
| Other revenue | |
| **TOTAL (5)** | |
| (6) ____________ | |
| Wages | ( ) |
| Utility | ( ) |
| Equipment rental | ( ) |
| Other variable expenses | ( ) |
| Fixed expenses / Overheads | ( ) |
| **TOTAL (6)** _________ | ( ) |
| **Tax owed** | ( ) |
| (7) ____________ | |

| (8) _________ | Month / Year (3) | Month / Year (2) | Month / Year (1) |
|---|---|---|---|
| **CASH RECEIPTS** | | | |
| Sales | | | |
| Loans | | | |
| Investments | | | |
| **TOTAL RECEIPTS** | | | |
| **DISBURSEMENTS** | | | |
| Salaries | | | |
| Advertising | | | |
| Insurance | | | |
| Overheads | | | |
| **TOTAL DISBURSEMENTS** | | | |
| **TOTAL RECEIPTS (less) DISBURSEMENTS** | | | |
| Effect of Exchange Rate Changes | | | |
| **NET INCREASE / DECREASE IN CASH & CASH EQUIVALENTS** | | | |

## F. CORPORATE FINANCE

***Find the synonym.***

• Production cost per unit item • Fixed costs • Wind up • Currency exchange rate • Person hour • Costing • Cash in hand • General expense • Cash inflow and outflow • Year-to-Date • Arrears • Operating expenses • To show a shortfall • Rate of return • Prediction • Operating profit margin • Revenue = expenses • Insolvency • Outgoings

**Overall expenses**

Overheads..................................................

Running costs ............................................

Expenditure ...............................................

Man-hour...................................................

Miscellaneous expense .................................

**Money matters**

Ready cash ................................................

Debt ..........................................................

Rate of exchange ........................................

Cash flow....................................................

**→ On the spreadsheet**

Forecast ..................................................

YTD......................................................

Break-even point .........................................

Unit cost ..................................................

Yield .......................................................

Cost analysis ..............................................

Operating margin .........................................

**Going under**

Bankruptcy ...............................................

Liquidate ..................................................

To show a loss ...........................................

***Do you know what a SWOT analysis is?***

## G. TAXATION

↘ ***Select the right word for the definition.***

**1.** A local tax on business.
**a)** Corporate tax **b)** Cooperation tax **c)** Professional tax

**2.** Tax people have to pay on their wages or salaries, and unearned income.
**a)** Revenue tax **b)** Salary tax **c)** Income tax

**3.** Tax imposed in some countries for a personal fortune.
**a)** Wealth tax **b)** Richness tax **c)** Fortune tax

**4.** Tax on profits from the sale of an asset.
**a)** Asset tax **b)** Capital gains tax **c)** Asset gains tax

**5.** Tax imposed on residential land.
**a)** Real estate tax **b)** Residence tax **c)** Land tax

**6.** A tax added at each stage of production or final stage which adds value.
**a)** Consumer tax **b)** Value added tax **c)** Consumption tax

**7.** Federal body for collecting most taxes.
**a)** Internal Revenue Service **b)** Federal Revenue Service **c)** Federal Tax Service

**8.** A country offering very favourable tax laws for foreigners.
**a)** Tax heaven **b)** Tax haven **c)** Tax paradise

**9.** A financial year for calculating yearly business statements.
**a)** Calculation year **b)** Financial statement year **c)** Fiscal year

**10.** Money back from the government when too much tax has been paid.
**a)** Tax rebate **b)** Tax return **c)** Tax reimbursement →

→ **11.** A form to fill out to declare your taxes.
**a)** Tax form **b)** Tax declaration **c)** Tax return

**12.** An unclear tax law which enables people to pay less tax.
**a)** Tax reduction **b)** Tax loophole **c)** Ambiguous tax

**13.** Deliberate and illegal failure to pay tax.
**a)** Tax evasion **b)** Tax default **c)** Fiscal fraud

**14.** Legally minimizing the amount of tax to be paid.
**a)** Creative taxing **b)** Minimal taxing **c)** Tax avoidance

**15.** A system by which tax on wages / salaries is retained at source.
**a)** W.R.A.S. **b)** P.A.Y.E. **c)** S.R.A.S.

## 2 Human Resources

### A. REMUNERATION

↘ ***Fill in the word puzzle (the first & last letters have been put in to help you).***

**1.** An employee benefit such as company car, expense account, etc.
**2.** Time worked more than contracted working hours, and paid extra!
**3.** The overall costs of paying all the employees in the company.
**4.** Whereby employees share some of the profits with the owners.
**5.** An unexpected extra for high productivity, seniority, incentive, etc.
**6.** An increase in wage or salary.
**7.** What you bring back home at the end of the week / month.
**8.** Pay calculated on an hourly rate / calculated on a monthly rate.
**9.** A coupon to pay for your lunch.
**10.** A reward system to give additional pay to workers.
**11.** Employee / employer social security contributions, pension plan, health insurance, etc.
**12.** The day you get paid.
**13.** Wages (in cash) enclosed in a (usually brown!) envelope on a weekly basis.
**14.** The right to buy a firm's stock at a stated price within a certain period of time.
**15.** One full-time job carried out by two people.
**16.** You "win" at the lottery, but you "e...." if you work.
**17.** A plan to prepare your retirement years.
**18.** The piece of paper telling you how much you have been paid, and listing deductions.
**19.** A prize given in recognition of exceptionally good work.
**20.** Wage multiplied by two for working, for example, on a Sunday or Public Holiday.
**Down:** An evaluation of job performance.

## B. THE RECRUITMENT PROCESS

*Complete the word chain with a verb and a noun.*

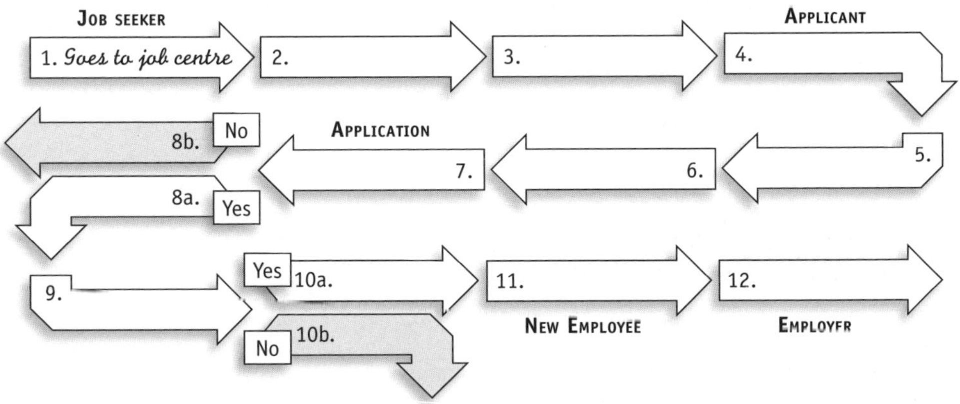


**Verb**

Goes to (1) – Applies for – Fills in – Turned down – Put on – Has – Writes up – Goes through – Gives – Put on – Looks at – Has – Appointed – Writes

**Noun**

Résumé (C.V.) – Screening process – Permanent part-time contract – Job adverts – Interview – For the job – Cover letter – Job centre (1) – Waiting list – A 3-month trial period – Application form – For the job – Short list – Job

## C. CLASSIFIED ADS

*Complete the job ads with one of the words below.*

- working knowledge
- qualifications
- hiring
- hard worker
- responsibilities
- experienced
- vacancy
- candidate
- work permit
- qualified
- applicant
- per annum
- background
- motivated team
- basic salary
- hands-on experience
- drive
- recruiting
- skills

DLM is ______ fork lift truck drivers for their logistics platform in Amsterdam. The _________ will have _____ __ __________ and be a ____ ______. For further information, please call +31 20 555 3121.

Total Transportation company is __________ ___________ truck drivers. Generous _____ ______+ overtime. ________________ include loading, unloading, basic maintenance and driving. International driver's license compulsory. Send C.V. by e-mail to totr@......

Are you a _________ P.A. with good secretarial and interpersonal ______? The right _________ will join a _________ ____ in this young headhunting company. _______ _________ of Italian is essential. Salary £18,000 ___ _____. Contact: Ann Other +44 2073 884 981.

Ideas Inc has a _______ for an ambitious permanent full-time engineer with _____ & enthusiasm to help set up a new industrialization department. We will get you a ____ ______ for the USA. Download application form on www.ideas.com.

Have you got an art-school __________? Do you have any graphic design ______________? We are looking for imaginative people to work in our nation-wide tourist brochure design department. Call Out-of-this-World Tours +61 7323 63893.

## D. YOU'VE GOT THE JOB!

*Complete each sentence using the phrases below.*

- you the position of Junior Consultant
- basis according to the contracts signed
- description and the terms and conditions of employment
- 25th January, 2010
- days a calendar month will accumulate as from your starting date
- Ms. Hopeful,
- to increase their monthly revenue
- please do not hesitate to contact my office
- period followed by a permanent full-time contract

- shall provide a relocation allowance
- coming to the interview in Los Angeles last week
- a starting salary of $5,050 per month
- in-house training and computer-based training programs
- your proficiency level
- 10 hours a day multiplied by the number of working days in a month

Dear ____________

*Thank you for ____________________________. We would like to offer ____________________________, commencing ____________________________.*
*You will have a statutory 6-month probationary ____________________________.*

*The rewards package includes____________________________,*
*to be increased according to ____________________________. You will also be paid commission on a percentage ____________________________,*
*and there is a payment by results scheme which enables you and your future colleagues ____________________________.*
*The contracted hours of work are the equivalent of ____________________________. Your leave entitlement (or paid leave) of 2 ____________________________.*
*Because you will be moving to the States, we ____________________________.*
*Career prospects and advancement are encouraged and we shall help you on the path to success with ____________________________.*
*Please find enclosed a job ____________________________, as well as the agreement for you to return signed, after reading attentively.*
*Should you require any further information, ____________________________.*

*Yours sincerely, James Joboffer, H.R. Manager*

## E. LEAVING OR LOSING A JOB

↘ *Find a headline in the snake below for each of the four short newspaper articles.*
*Sacked for Professional Misconduct Redundancy plan No more merit bonuses $500,000 Golden Handshake for C.E.O.*

1. .......................................
"We just have to reduce our headcount," said the HR Manager last week. 40 members of staff will be laid off, but they will be retrained with an eye to reorientation and new job openings. There is also a generous severance pay. "We have created a special outplacement service to help with job hunting. Labour shedding is difficult for all of us but we plan to leave no one jobless". It's better than closure.

2. .......................................!
After 55 years of loyal service, Ham Weary took early retirement last week. "I'm burnt out, and just want to enjoy myself now." And he can, given the generous pension he will receive! "That's a record length of service but we were still surprised when he handed in his notice," said a colleague.

3. .......................................
"It was a dead end job and I was about to quit anyway," said Peter Sackville. While I'm between jobs, I shall have some vocational training, do an internship somewhere, and find something much more interesting. I'm glad I was fired and I only nicked a few tools after all!"

4. .......................................
Senior executives went on strike last week after they had been informed that merit ratings were no longer to be used to increase their revenue. Several executives were also demoted in an effort to get company finance back on track. Further investigation showed that the root of the problem was, however, that two junior executives had been promoted, and their salaries increased accordingly.

## F. LABOUR RELATIONS

↘ *Un-jumble the words to find the answer to the clue.*

**Possible causes of labour unrest:**

**1.** A period in which the number of working hours is reduced
hrosrt mtei ogrwkin → ..........................................................................................

**2.** Termination of an employment contract for unfounded reasons
nifuar ssdmislia → .................................................................................... →

→ **3.** Intimidation of a weaker person to make them do something
ybnuligl → ..........................................................................................................

**4.** Intimidation of a sexual nature
leusax amerasthsn → ..........................................................................................

**5.** An inadequate number of workers or employees
dnfestuardfe → ..................................................................................................

**6.** The smallest hourly wage which can be legally paid
inmummi gaew → ..............................................................................................

**Which can lead to industrial strife:**

**7.** Formal notice of employee dissatisfaction
arieevgnc → .......................................................................................................

**8.** Disagreement between employer and workers
pistedu → ..........................................................................................................

**9.** Someone who stirs up trouble on purpose
rbutleo krmae → ...............................................................................................

**10.** Labour participating in company decision making
orrwek eptrneseinator → ...................................................................................

**11.** A temporary work stoppage caused by an unsolved complaint
irkset → .............................................................................................................

**12.** A line of people staging a protest (often during 11.)
cktpei inle → ....................................................................................................

**13.** A worker who crosses (12) and goes into work
bcas → ...............................................................................................................

**14.** A (11) in which workers leave the premises
kuawolt → .........................................................................................................

**Management complaints:**

**15.** During the hours someone is paid for
ni moypcna item → ............................................................................................

**16.** Habitual failure to appear for work
nbsetemaeis → .................................................................................................

**And to find a solution:**

**17.** To act between parties to find a solution
trbiaater → ........................................................................................................

**18.** An organisation of workers to defend their interests
oablru nniuo → .................................................................................................

**19.** A committee formed of workers and employer
oksrw oinculc → ................................................................................................

**20.** Synonym for labour law
aoblru doce → ...................................................................................................

**21.** Decision-making process between employer and workers
vocletliec agigbairnn → ....................................................................................

## 3 I.T. (Information Technology)

### A. COMPUTER KEYWORDS

*Match the question to the answer.*

1. What is Plug-and-Play?
2. What on earth is a smart card?
3. What do you usually need to access a company computer?
4. What's the name of the device which manages a computer resource?
5. Which part of the keyboard has 4 rows of numbers on it (on laptops just 1)?
6. When you activate a process from a distance, what do you use?
7. What does digital technology mean?

- **A.** A server
- **B.** The use of the binary system – 0 or 1 – off or on (as opposed to the analog system)
- **C.** A computer system which works as soon as it is connected
- **D.** A numeric pad
- **E.** Remote control
- **F.** A plastic card containing a microprocessor
- **G.** A password

### B. HARDWARE

*Match the PC (Personal Computer) component on the list to the picture.*

• CD drive • Keyboard • Screen/monitor/VDU (Visual Display Unit) • Mouse • Printer • Scanner
• CPU (Central Processing Unit) • USB flash drive / key

1. ..................................
2. ..................................
3. ..................................
4. ..................................
5. ..................................
6. ..................................
7. ..................................
8. ..................................

## C. SOFTWARE

↘ ***Put a word from the list into the right place in the text.***

• Word processing • Computer programs • Computer games • Desk Top Publishing • Operating System • Educational software • Computer memory • Presentation software • Database Management • Driver software • Media player • Bit / Byte / Megabyte / Gigabyte • Data

Generally speaking, **(1)** c.................... m.................... (often now known as RAM) includes the devices where **(2)** d.................... or **(3)** c.................... p.................... are stored.
This RAM and the hard disk capacity are measured in **(4)** b.................... / b.................... / m.................... and g.................... .
The **(5)** O.................... S.................... (O.S.) allows the hardware to work properly.
Different kinds of software include:
Software for entertainment: **(6)** c.................... g....................
Programs so the computer can interact with hardware: **(7)** d.................... s....................
Software designed for playing music and videos or films: **(8)** m.................... p....................
Productive software for: **(9)** d.................... m.................... ; w.................... p...................., DTP (d.................... t.................... p....................) and p.................... s....................
And finally, programs for teaching: **(10)** e.................... s....................

## D. SURFING THE WEB (By a novice!)

↘ ***Firstly – put your computer into English! Then try putting these sentences into the right order.***

**1)**A → **2)**________ → **3)**________ → **4)**________ → **5)**________ → **6)**________ →
**7)**________ → **8)**________ → **9)**________ → **10)**________ → **11)**________ → **12)**________

**A.** First of all, you'll need a browser (a software program) to search for information.
**B.** Choose the right link to go to another page.
**C.** Don't forget to log off.
**D.** You'll get onto the home page.
**E.** You'll also need an Internet Service Provider (or ISP) for Internet access.
**F.** Type in the key words – press enter.
**G.** If you like this page, you can bookmark it for another day.
**H.** Once you are on-line, you can use the network (or World Wide Web).
**I.** Choose a website among the selection – press enter.
**J.** Download the information or software you need onto your computer.
**K.** Log on if the website is protected.
**L.** Choose a search engine

## E. COMPUTER PROBLEMS

*Match the complaint to the solution.*

1. My computer has crashed / frozen. •
2. I seem to have a virus. •
3. I'm worried about computer fraud. •
4. My computer seems to output the wrong thing. •
5. I'm worried about a hacker getting into my computer. •
6. My computer cannot run the new program I bought. •

- **a.** Re-check what you have put into your computer. Of course, the output depends on the input. In other words, if you input rubbish, you output rubbish or.... GIGO (Garbage in – garbage out)
- **b.** Write down the error message, re-start your computer, cross your fingers. If all fails, call a computer expert.
- **c.** Use every kind of computer protection possible – anti-virus, firewall, make sure your o.s. is up to date and keep track of what is happening on your system.
- **d.** You need to upgrade your computer.
- **e.** Be careful about who has access to your computer and buy a system to protect your computer against anything with a bug coming in.
- **f.** Thieves and criminals must be stopped. Delete unsolicited e-mails and pop-ups, and never send sensitive information through unsecured e-mails.

## F. I HAD NO INTERNET CONNECTION!!

*Put the right word in the gap.*

• ethernet cable • P2P applications • wireless • re-boot • high speed internet access • bandwidth hog • wall jack

1. I needed ....................
2. I wanted to use my WIFI but was too far away from the AP to use ...................
3. I had to use an ...................
4. Which I plugged into a ....................
5. This had no effect, so I had to ................... my computer.
6. In fact another program was a ................... and disrupted my connection.
7. Conclusion: Beware of ...................!

***Don't forget to backup your data!!***

## G. 5 CONFUSING WORDS

*Make the right choice (you may have to put the verb in the right tense).*

**1. Actually/currently: a)** I ............... think you ought to take some time off.
**b)** They are ............... working on a new design.
**2. Advice/advise: a)** The lawyer ............... us to read the small print.
**b)** You should listen to his ................
**3. Assure / ensure / insure: a)** To ............... product quality, we have added self-inspection.
**b)** Be sure to ............. your valuables. **c)** Let me ............... you that I will be on time.
**4. Control / inspect / check: a)** Could you just ............... these goods before dispatch?
**b)** Each item is carefully ................ before it leaves the assembly line.
**c)** Overall quality ............... is part of our company policy.
**5. Beside / besides: a)** ............... me who thinks we should lay off 10 direct workers?
**b)** Why don't we put the scanner ............ the desktop?

# 4 Logistics

## A. IN THE WAREHOUSE

*Put the sentences in a logical order in the right box.*

**RECEPTION / INCOMING GOODS**

**WAREHOUSE / STOREHOUSE / STOREROOM /STOCKROOM**

**DISPATCH / SHIPPING**

Unload & unpack the goods
Deliver the goods to the customer
Use a fork lift truck / hand pallet truck to handle the goods
Sign the delivery note
Make up the order and package the goods
Stack the raw materials / part assemblies / purchased parts / finished products on the rack
Dispatch the finished product
Check the raw materials / part assemblies / purchased parts, on arrival from the supplier / sub-contractor

## B. STOCK MANAGEMENT / STORAGE TIPS FOR THE WAREHOUSEMAN / STOCK KEEPER

↘ *Put the following words into the right gap.*

• reminder • delivery deadlines • stocklist (GB) / inventory (USA) • FIFO • out of stock • delivery delay • shortage • stocktaking • lead time • stock-in-hand

**a)** Calculate the .............................. .............................. to give a delivery date.
**b)** Check the customer's .............................. .............................. for outgoing goods.
**c)** Warn customer of a .............................. .............................. .
**d)** Use .............................. (First in – first out) Management tools.
**e)** Take stock to avoid a .............................. / lack of incoming goods.
**f)** Check the .............................. in your warehouse.
**g)** Send a .............................. to the supplier about the remainder of the order.
**h)** Re-order goods before being .............................. .............................. .............................. .
**i)** Update your .............................. .
**j)** Once a month / year, do the inventory / .............................. .

## C. WHAT'S ON THE STICKER?

↘ *Match one word from column A with one word from column B.*

| A: | B: |
|---|---|
| Expiry • | • code |
| Handle • | • tag |
| Hazardous • | • date |
| RFID (Radio-Frequency Identification) • | • materials |
| Quality • | • number |
| Bar • | • with care |
| Batch • | • control label |

## D. FREIGHT TRANSPORTATION (USA) / TRANSPORT of GOODS (UK)

↘ *Put the following words into the right balloon.*

• Regulations • Shipment notice • Haulage company handling charges • Goods in bond • Border • Haulier freight rate • Consignment note • Customs clearance documents • Duty • Air waybill • Freight forwarder invoice • Prohibited goods • Bonded warehouse • Carrier loading charges • Certificate of origin • Packing list

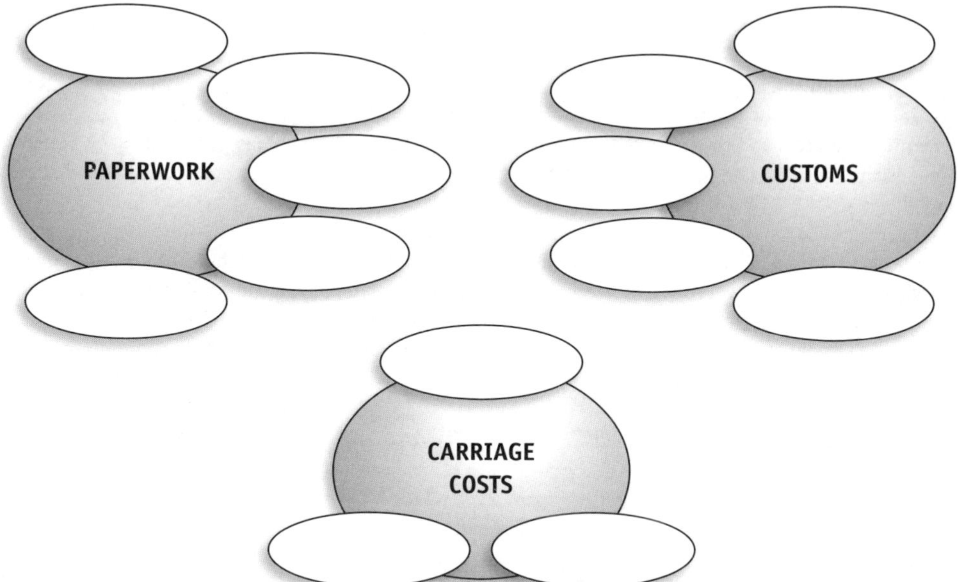


## E. GOODS IN TRANSIT

↘ *Make pairs (homonyms, synonyms...). E.g.: Lorry (UK) – Truck (USA)*

• Lorry (UK) • Cubic capacity • FCL (Full container load) • Truck (USA) • Carriage by sea • HGV (Heavy goods vehicle) • RORO (roll on roll off) • Scheduled time of departure • Part load • Trucker • Delivery van • Time of arrival • Rail transport • Driver • Trailer • Net weight

.....................................................................................................................................

.....................................................................................................................................

.....................................................................................................................................

# 5 Maintenance

## A. WHAT A WEEK!

↘ *Replace the underlined word in the text with another underlined word so that it makes sense.*

We have had a lot of problems recently. Just take a look at this report:
Monday: Electricity – we had a <u>machine failure</u> / ............................ so there was no <u>malfunction</u> / .................................. to the machines.
Tuesday: Severe <u>Neglect</u> / ....................... . We had to put <u>"sudden failure"</u> / ......................→

→ signs up on them all – and just before a customer audit! The <u>wear</u> / ................................. (quite unexpected) of the punching machine caused the most <u>anomaly</u>/ ................................., when the operators had to sit around doing nothing while the equipment was out of use.
Wednesday: Time to sort out the reasons for <u>backlog</u>/ .................................. This is what we found:
<u>out of order</u>/ .............................. – some parts had just been progressively worn away.
<u>overload</u> / .............................. – some of the machines had not been looked after well enough.
<u>power supply</u>/ .......................... – we cannot repair the material and will need to order new parts.
Thursday: Electricity <u>machine breakdowns</u>/ ................................. – this time too much energy!
There seems to be an <u>downtime</u>/ ............................. in the system, something is not quite right.
You can just imagine the <u>power cut</u> / ................................. we have now – really late compared with our schedule!
Friday: T.G.I.F. if there is a <u>Core damage</u>/ ................................. over the weekend, someone else will have to mend it.

## B. PREVENTION IS BETTER THAN CURE!

↘ ***Answer the clues to fill the word puzzle and find the hidden word.***

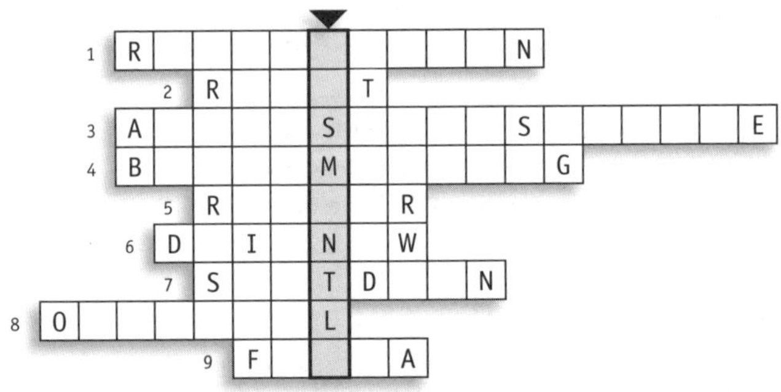


**1.** To put back in a good condition
**2.** Requip
**3.** The service from a supplier after you have bought their goods
**4.** Continual research for new ideas, methods, practises and processes by comparison
**5.** To mend, fix, or ...........
**6.** D.I.N. – non emergency work which has to be done immediately (usually for the boss!)
**7.** Outage (downtime) scheduled in advance for maintenance
**8.** A full examination and restoration of equipment
**9.** Failure Modes Effects and Criticality Analysis (acronym)
**Hidden word:** To take apart

# 6 Management

## A. BUSINESS PLANNING

***Find the synonym(s) and complete the speech with the words in the right-hand column.***

profitability – in the short / medium / long run – half – cost effective – goal – anticipate – forecast – outcome – compulsory – second semester – target – guidelines – first quarter – aim – corporate strategy

| | | |
|---|---|---|
| 1. | Objective | |
| 2. | The first 3 months of the year | |
| 3. | The second six months of the year | |
| 4. | Result | |
| 5. | Guiding principle | |
| 6. | Prediction / projection | |
| 7. | Short / medium / long term | |
| 8. | Obligatory | |
| 9. | Company policy | |
| 10. | The ability to generate revenue | |
| 11. | Cost efficient | |
| 12. | Foresee or foreknow | |

Ladies and gentlemen. Thank you for coming at such short notice. First please take a look at the f.................... for the f.................... q.................... 20--. Our t.................... is to make production more c.................... e.................... so that by the end of the s.................... s.................... of the year, we will have increased our p.................... – to the delight of the shareholders of course. To this end, we have written up new g.................... with both optional and c.................... changes to be made by each department head.

The main change to our c.................... s.................... is to a.................... any market changes way ahead of the competition, and thus become leaders in our market sector. Of course, in the short term this will involve a lot of extra work, but in the l.................... r.................... it means jobs and profits for everyone!!

## B. AN OVERPAID MANAGER

***A typical manager...***

| | |
|---|---|
| **1.** Handles a heavy W_ _ _ _ _ _ D | RALODOKW |
| **2.** Is snowed under by P _ _ _ _ _ _ _ K | RAKWOEPRP |
| **3.** Has a good B _ _ _ _ _ _S S _ _ _ E | NSUSEISB ESENS |
| **4.** Is not always on the same W _ _ _ _ _ _ _ _ H | EWELNVGTHA |
| **5.** Is I _ _ _ _ _ _ D in every part of the business | VEVLDNOI |
| **6.** M _ _ _ _ _ _ _ _ _ S operations and solutions | AETRSDNMIMS |
| **7.** Relies on F _ _ _ _ _ _ K to take decisions | EECBFKAD |
| **8.** Underlines key factors in C _ _ _ _ _ _ _ E S _ _ _ _ _ _ Y | RTOERAPOC TASETYGR |
| **9.** Gives out information on a N_ _ D-TO-K _ _W basis | EEND TO NWOK |
| **10.** Is usually B _ _ _ _ _ _ _ _ _ _ E | UEEKLBISNISS |
| **11.** Trusts in A _ _ _ _ _ _ _ _ _ _ Y for effective change management | ADAPYLBTIAIT |
| **12.** Claims to be O _ _ _ _ _ _ _ _ D & U _ _ _ _ _ _ _ D | RVWREKOEOD & NEAUDIPDR |

## C. RUNNING A COMPANY

*Match the word to the definition – in the right column of course!*

• Tackle a problem • Fall short of forecasts • Goodwill • The pros and cons • MBO (Management by objectives) • Teamwork • Ideas box • Sensitive issue • Leadership • Be aware • Shortfall in earnings • Mediate

| MANAGEMENT TOOLS | ROADS TO IMPROVEMENT | PROBLEMS TO BRING UP |
|---|---|---|
| Reward staff if results are close to objectives .<br>1. ....................................... | An intangible asset – staff morale, a good reputation...<br>5. ....................................... | A rather thorny problem, which might make waves.<br>9. ....................................... |
| Team up with the right colleagues.<br>2. ....................................... | A place to suggest initiatives anonymously.<br>6. ....................................... | The upsides (for) and the downsides (against).<br>10. ....................................... |
| Influence people to reach the right target.<br>3. ....................................... | To undertake to find the solution to a quandary.<br>7. ....................................... | Not making as much money as expected.<br>11. ....................................... |
| Reconcile, resolve or settle differences.<br>4. ....................................... | Be in the know of openings for the future.<br>8. ....................................... | Anything which is not up to what was predicted.<br>12. ....................................... |

## D. CORPORATE GOVERNANCE AND ETHICS

*Find the antonym to have some* **CORE VALUES.** *The number of dashes = the number of letters.*

**1.** Someone who doesn't tell the truth // Someone who is T __ __ __ __ __ __ __ __

**2.** Someone who is unfair // Someone who is F __ __ __

**3.** Someone who is dishonest // Someone who is H __ __ __ __ __

**4.** Someone who has no moral integrity // Someone who is D __ __ __ __ __ __

**5.** Someone who has no principles of right or wrong // Someone who is M __ __ __ __

**6.** Someone who doesn't respect the law // Someone who does things which are L __ __ __ __

*Add consonants to make the* **3 Rs.**

| | |
|---|---|
| **7.** __ E __ __ E __ __ | High regard or consideration |
| __ E __ __ O __ __ I __ I __ I __ __ | Moral, legal or mental accountability |
| __ E __ U __ __ __ | The consequences of an action |

*Match the beginning to the end of the expression to find an* **ETHICAL CODE.**

| | |
|---|---|
| **8.** Environmental • | • products and services to customers |
| **9.** Fairness • | • local communities |
| **10.** Accountability to • | • rate of return for investors |
| **11.** Providing responsible • | • towards employees |
| **12.** Maintaining a healthy • | • responsibility |

## SAFETY FIRST!

↘ *Choose a) or b) each time.*

**MEMORANDUM: To all factory employees**

Following a safety assessment, it has come to our notice that certain rules are not being respected. In order to comply with **1/** *(a) Regulatory requirements (b) Rule requirements* we would like to re-iterate the following guidelines:

**Fire hazards:**
Danger symbols and codes are to be used for **2/** *(a) flammable (b) non-flammable* or explosive products.
Fireproof partitions are to be installed around fire hazards.
A lightning protection device is to be installed on the roof.
The **3/** *(a) alarm (b) bell* is to be tested on a daily basis.
Fire-fighting appliances **4/** (*(a) fire extincters (b) fire extinguishers* etc. are to be clearly marked and easily accessible.
24/7 easy access for fire-service vehicles (i.e. traffic lanes and driveways are to be kept clear).

**Waste water treatment:**
Unpolluted rainwater is to be recycled.
The **5/** *(a) water tightness (b) waterproofness* of retention tanks is to be checked monthly.
**6/** *(a) Release (b) Spillage* and leak risk assessment to be carried out monthly to avoid pollutant escape.
The sanitation network is to be regularly checked for suitable sewage disposal.

**Hazardous products:**
The level **7/** *(a) gauger (b) gauge* is to be checked weekly.
Be **8/** *(a) cautions (b) prudent* when using certain products.
Monthly measurements, samples and analysis of air emissions (gas, fumes, particles) are to be recorded.

**Employee well-being and safety:**
The working environment is to be well-ventilated and suitably lit.
Each worker is to be supplied with material for individual protection in personal lockers – one-piece **9/** *(a) cover-ups (b) coveralls*, autonomous breathing apparatus, boots, product-resistant gloves.
Each worker is responsible for **10/** *(a) self-control (b) self-monitoring of tools and machinery*.
Each machine is to be fitted with safety guards and an **11/** *(a) urgency stop button (b) emergency stop button* (dead man's switch).
There will be a weekly **12/** *(a) fire drill (b) fire routine* on each shift.
The level of noise emission is to be monitored.
A qualified **13/** *(a) First saver (b) First aider* is to be available during working hours in case of an accident.
As from now on, there will be regular **14/** *(a) check-ups (b) spot checks*.
A description of **15/** *(a) non-compliance (b) non-respect* will be sent to head office.

**Remember: CARELESSNESS COSTS LIVES.**

## 1 Marketing & Advertising

### A. THE MARKETING MIX

↘ ***Fill in the vowels to find the 4 Ps.***

PR__D__CT * PR__C__ * PL__C__ * PR__M__T__ __N

### B. A MARKETING BRIEF

↘ ***Replace the phrase in italics with a suitable word from the list below.***

Market research • Marketing brief • Market trend • Eye-catching packaging • Target market • Jingle • Brand awareness • A non-starter • O.T.S. • Launch • Opinion poll • Product range

**Bill:** Right, everyone, as you know, we have been given a (**1.** *The instructions before we begin the project*) ........................................ by Chummy Chocs, pet food suppliers. I'm afraid that I reckon the product is (**2.** *Something with no chance of success*) ........................................

**Bob:** Well, I must say that the company needs to extend its (**3.** *All the types of product made by one company*) ................................................ – they have only produced traditional pet food up to now. They need to adjust their offer to the current (**4.** *Tendency of the market*) ........................................

**Bill:** And what might that be?

**Bob:** Well, people are spoiling their pets more and more. For this product, the (**5.** *Market segment for a particular product*) ........................................ is the top of the range, people with money to spare.

**Bill:** So you're talking about the high price bracket?

**Bob:** That's right.

**Jill:** Could I just come in here? I think we ought to do some market analysis before we go any further. Maybe we could carry out an (**6.** *An enquiry into public opinion*) ........................................ in the poodle parlours (grooming saloons) and outside up-market pet food stores.

**Bill:** That sounds like a good idea to me. Can you get back to me within a fortnight?

.....

3 weeks later:

**Bill:** So, what was the result of the (**7.** *Collection and analysis of data*) ..................................?

**Jill:** Well, there is certainly room for the product on the market. It is up to us to create a need and convince the buyer that this is just the product they want.

**Bob:** That's great. I like this product (I'll certainly use it myself – can I have some free samples?!).

**Bill:** Let's get back to business. My first question is – what are the alternative kinds of distribution we can use?

→

→ **Jill:** Well, I was thinking of selling in pet supply stores mainly. Of course, we could do some direct selling on-line as well.
Then we need to think of the (**8.** *How many people will have the opportunity to see the product*) ..........................................., so we should have some in-store promotions too.
**Bob:** We could have a widespread publicity campaign for (**9.** *The level of brand recognition*) ............................................ too.
**Jill:** I think we need some (**10.** *Wrapping which you cannot miss*) ............................................ – I'll get the marketing team onto that, and then a slogan like "chummy chocs for your best chum", or a catchphrase like "yummy chummy".
**Bob:** Yes, and a logo – I have an idea for that – look!
**Jill:** The (**11.** *Catchy, musical advertising slogan*) ............................................ could remind people of the noise dogs make when they're happy – what noise do they make when they're happy?
**Bob:** This is all so exciting!
**Bill:** Then I suppose all we have to do is (**12.** *Start to put*) ............................................ the product on the market?!! And hope it's in high demand!

## C. WHICH WORD SHOULD I USE?

*Match the word to the definition.*

| | |
|---|---|
| **1.** Advertising • | • **A.** A small ad |
| **2.** Publicity • | • **B.** Asks for opinions |
| **3.** Market research • | • **C.** A small book, like a pamphlet |
| **4.** Marketing research • | • **D.** Publicity you pay for |
| **5.** Survey • | • **E.** A small, top-of-the-market sector |
| **6.** Opinion poll • | • **F.** One-page advertising (can be a throw-away) |
| **7.** Market trend • | • **G.** The study of how a product will sell |
| **8.** Market forecast • | • **H.** What will exist in the future |
| **9.** Niche market • | • **I.** A large billboard for advertising |
| **10.** Mass market • | • **J.** What exists at the current time |
| **11.** A classified ad • | • **K.** With this, you get a free sample |
| **12.** A spread • | • **L.** A market available to everyone |
| **13.** A hoarding • | • **M.** A full page or double page ad |
| **14.** A poster • | • **N.** General research – media, economic climate, etc. |
| **15.** A leaflet • | • **O.** You get something which has been pre-paid |
| **16.** A booklet • | • **P.** A large-format print for advertising |
| **17.** A coupon • | • **Q.** Asks for statistics, numbers to be analysed |
| **18.** A voucher • | • **R.** Publicity which is free |

## D. DIFFERENT KINDS OF PROMOTION & ADVERTISING (or ADVERT, or AD!)

***Match the conversation to the kind of promotion.***

**A.** It says "fill in the card and send it back for more information".

**B.** I heard about it between the news and the film on channel 2.

**C.** This printed product gives us all the information we need to choose our holiday.

***D.** This is a special offer to introduce you to our new shampoo.*

**E.** Would you like to take this leaflet to read more about our organic food ?

**F.** Don't buy our competitor's pasta, you know it's not good for you.

***G.** Look at that man walking down the street with burgers on his back!*

**H.** Shall we go to the agricultural show next week?

**I.** Let's send out information through the post.

**J.** Let's put lots of our products in the shop window.

**K.** Look, this one comes with a free sample!

***L.** A friend told me about "wonder" washing powder.*

**1.** Handout
**2.** Mail shot / direct mail advertising
**3.** Radio commercial / TV commercial
**4.** Word of mouth
**5.** Sandwich board man
**6.** Introductory offer
**7.** A freebie / a giveaway
**8.** A reply card
**9.** Trade fair – Boat / car show
**10.** Shop frontage
**11.** Brochure
**12.** Know-better advertising

## E. LET'S GIVE SALES A BOOST

***Guess what? – Complete the word puzzle and find one thing which makes for good sales.***

**1.** A cabinet to show your goods in
**2.** A brief publicity statement (like on the back of a book)
**3.** A payable public promotion
**4.** A person whose business is advertising
**5.** The amount broadcast in the media
**6.** When the biggest audience watches the TV
**7.** Audience measurement
**8.** Make an impact on the public by teasing them
**9.** A cabinet to display your goods in
**10.** A room to show your goods in
**11.** Consumer commitment to one brand
**12.** A card issued by stores to reward regular customers (by points)
**13.** A small book
**14.** The fourth word in the Marketing Mix
**15.** Text of an advertising message

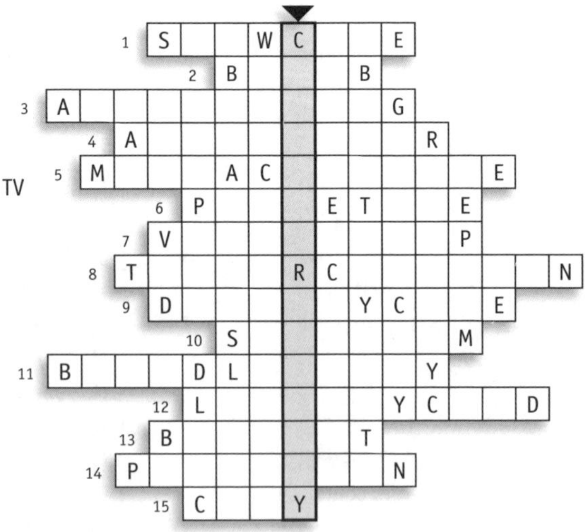

## A. PRODUCT FEATURES IN ALL SHAPES AND SIZES

↘ ***Replace the word in italics with one or more of the words below.***

• Taken the place of • Custom-made • Lid • Own brand label • Sell-by date • No-brand articles • Good value for money • Fake • Produce • Throw-away • Cordless • Foodstuffs • Lifespan • Shoddy • Tamper-proof / airtight / refillable / self-locking

**1.** Of course, these are *disposable nappies / diapers USA* .................... – they can be put in the bin.
**2.** That is not the real thing – it's a *forgery* ............................
**3.** These goods are really *trashy* ............................ – not good quality at all.
**4.** Could you tell me where the *groceries section* ............................ is, please?
**5.** Look at the price of those *made-to-measure* ............................ shoes!
**6.** You can relax while you watch – no need to move – it's operated by *remote control* ....................
**7.** It's a *private label brand (PLB)* .............. – the store's own brand – we prefer to sell what we know.
**8.** This state-of-the-art radio has a very good *quality-price ratio* ............................
**9.** In this area of the store are the *edible products* ............................
**10.** Make sure that you check the *best before date* ............................
**11.** This model has *superseded* .................. the former model, of course, with improved performance.
**12.** We can supply all kinds of packaging to suit your needs – such as *watertight* ........................
**13.** Make sure the *top* .................... is on tight.
**14.** We have to make sure how long the product will last – the *shelf life* ....................
**15.** Over there are *the no-name goods* .................... – the ones without a brand name.

## B. THE BARE NECESSITIES

↘ ***Think about the answer!***

**A: 1.** Something made by people.
**2.** Something made by a machine.
**3.** Something made my hand.

**a)** Handmade
**b)** Machine-made
**c)** Man-made

**B: 1.** Parts which can be taken out.
**2.** Parts which replace a faulty part.

**a)** Spare parts
**b)** Removable parts

**C: 1.** Basic necessities such as milk, bread...
**2.** Something you buy because you suddenly want to.

**a)** Staple goods
**b)** Impulse purchase

**D: 1.** Goods which have a limited lifespan, such as food, medicine, etc.
**2.** Goods which last for several years, such as washing machines, washing-up machines, etc.

**a)** Consumer durables
**b)** Perishable goods

**E: 1.** Something which doesn't cost a lot.
**2.** Something which costs a lot.

**a)** Inexpensive
**b)** Costly

**F: 1.** An item which is not completely finished.
**2.** The final, finished product.

**a)** End product
**b)** Semi-finished goods

**G: 1.** The person who will actually use the item.
**2.** The person responsible for selling the item.

**a)** Seller
**b)** End-user

## C. 6 MORE CONFUSING WORDS

*Same as always!*

**1. Downside / underside: a)** The ............... of each piece is carefully finished.
**b)** The ............... of the situation is the extra work it implies.
**2. Hard / hardly: a)** We ............... have time to get them finished before the deadline.
**b)** Could you please work ........... to finish on time?
**3. Lay down / lie down: a)** They ............... the rules for working hours.
**b)** My company is so caring – there is even a place to ............... and rest!
**4. Raise / rise: a)** The C.E.O. from the States is coming, please ............. to the occasion.
**b)** Oh no! They're going to ............... taxes again!
**5. Remind / remember: a)** ............... me about the meeting, won't you?
**b)**................ to fill in the form overleaf.
**6. Wins / earns: a)** He ............... 24,000 dollars a month.
**b)** He ............... 200,000 dollars on the lottery.

# 3 Production

## A. ON THE FACTORY FLOOR

*Put the words into the right balloon.*

• cleanroom • stoppage • J.I.T.P. (Just in time production) • foreman • wastage • mechanic • process costing • workshop • lean production • bottleneck • changing room • self-inspection • workmate • restricted area • backlog • safety instructions • setter • rework area for defective products or customization

## B. A PRODUCTION PROCESS FLOWCHART

↘ ***Put the following information in the right place on the flowchart.***

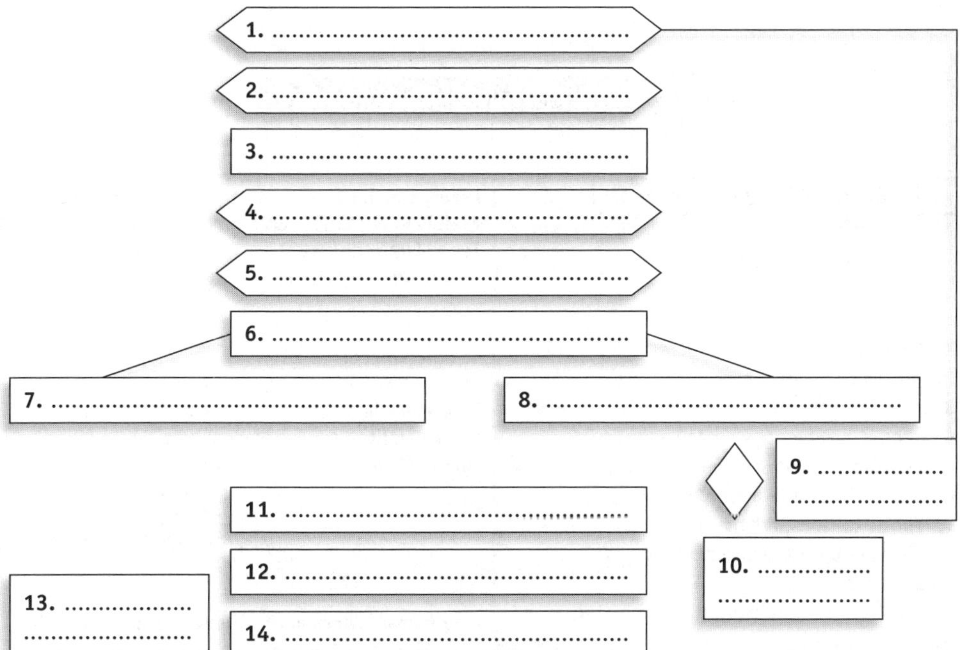


Initiate / launch production run – Make as many by-products as possible – Prepare machine tools / tooling – Shrinkwrap goods before dispatch – Continue – Do pilot / test run – Work in progress / work in hand – Purchase raw materials and purchased parts (outsourced / subcontracted) – Keep waste and scrap to a minimum – Deliver part assemblies / subsets / semi-processed goods to the assembly line – Write up work orders and standard work – Better do Value Stream Mapping! – Prepare product schedule / planning / routing – Smooth assembly process with no idle capacity time

## C. HATEFUL HOMONYMS

*Try your luck.*

**1. Facts / fax: a)** Did you get the ............... I sent yesterday?
**b)** Have you got the ............... right?
**2. Leased / least: a)** At ................ you could have waited for me!
**b)** He has ................ the premises for 3 years.
**3. Principal / principle: a)** The ............... is that happy operatives are efficient.
**b)** The ............... idea is to get everyone motivated.
**4. Right / write: a)** Have you got the ................ or wrong answer?
**b)** Have you got time to ............... to the supplier?
**5. Stationary / stationery: a)** There's no more paper! Who orders the ..............?
**b)** I don't know how those soldiers stay ............... for so long.
**6. By / bye / buy: a)** ............... for now!
**b)** ............... the way, did you know that...?
**c)** ............... now and pay in 3 months!

# 4 Purchasing & Procurement

## A. PURCHASING PAPERWORK

*Look at the three documents, and answer the questions below.*

**1.** What goods have been ordered?
**2.** How much do they cost each?
**3.** When was the order confirmed?
**4.** When will the goods be delivered?
**5.** Will all the goods be delivered on that date?
**6.** How much do the goods weigh?
**7.** Who is to transport the goods?
**8.** What are the particular packing requirements?
**9.** How long after delivery do Illuminated Interiors have to pay for the goods?
**10.** Where will the goods be delivered?

**Luxury Lighting Ltd**
**43 Bulb Way, LIGHTSTEAD**
**Tel: +44 (0) 1675 756 638**
**E-mail: orders@LLL.com**

**DELIVERY NOTE**
No._3006________
Illuminated Interiors
Lamp Lane, London
**DELIVERY ADDRESS**
_Same as above___
________________

Your References:
Order: 1376 Date: 21/02/20..
Customer No.: 5371
Customer: Ill. Int.
Your Contact:

**ILL REFERENCES**
Shipping Date: 01/04/20..
Delivery Conditions:
Attn: FRAGILE
Delivery Terms: Ex-works
Order No.: 1376 Date: 21/02/20..
Salesperson: Sparky Bright

| Line | Item n° | EAN Code | Qty Delivered | Remaining Qty |
|---|---|---|---|---|
| 1 | IPE/203 | 333484836573 | 3 boxes | 2 boxes |

| | |
|---|---|
| Number of packages: | 3 |
| Number of pallets: | 1 |
| Carrier: | Take-it-away Bros. |
| Gross Weight: | 5.6 kg |
| Volume: | 4.00 m² |

Any complaint concerning this delivery is to be addressed to the company within 72 hours stating the Delivery Note Number and the Item Number.

**ILLUMINATED INTERIORS** **PURCHASE ORDER**
**LAMP LANE, LONDON**
**Tel: +44 (0) 1271 383 4644**
**E-mail: information@ILLINT.com**

Order Number: 1376 Date: 21/02/20..
Supplier: Customer A/C No.: 5371
Luxury Lighting Ltd, 43 Bulb Way, LIGHTSTEAD
Postcode: SW3 5ME
Country: U.K.
Tel: +44(0)1675 756 638
E-mail: orders@LLL.com
Delivery address: Same as above

| ITEM | REF No. | Colour/Size | UNIT PRICE | QTY | € |
|---|---|---|---|---|---|
| Lights | IP3./203 | Red/Large | 5.00 | 100 | 500 |

TOTAL PAYMENT DUE __500€_____

Please send order confirmation to above address

**ORDER CONFIRMATION**
Created on: 28/02/20.. Revised : 01/03/20..
Printed on: 01/03/20.. Page: 1 Of: 1

Customer :
Illuminated Interiors
_Lamp Lane, London_

Delivery address:
___Same________

Our VAT No.: 83154574883
Your VAT No.: 76501 392988
Contact: Sparky Bright
Tel. No.: 1087 338 555
Forwarding Agent: Take-it-away Bros
Packing: FRAGILE – bubble-wrap

Your Order No.: 1376
Terms of payment: 30 days upon receipt of goods
Customs Code: XXY
Incoterm: Ex-works
Goods rendered: Customer

| Description | Delivery Date | Quantity | Unit Price | Total |
|---|---|---|---|---|
| Lights | 01/04/20.. | 100 | 5.00 | 500.00 |

## B. PURCHASING PARTS OR ORDERING FROM A SERVICE PROVIDER (Electricity, Internet, Telephone, etc.)

*Put the sentences below into the right place in the flowdiagram.*

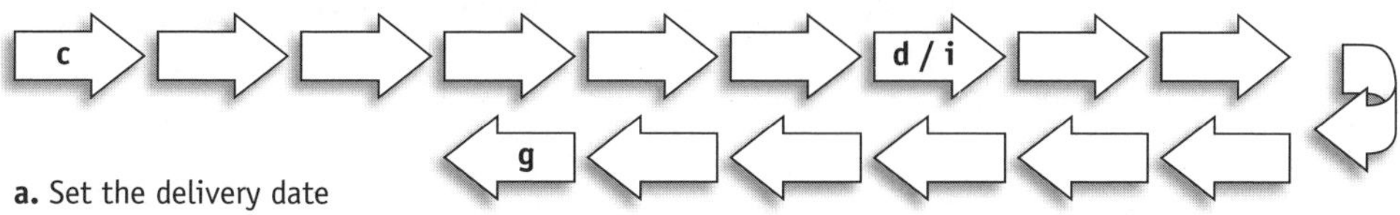


**a.** Set the delivery date
**b.** Negotiate the terms and conditions
**c.** Decide whether to supply in-house / in-plant or to outsource / sub-contract
**d.** Check the lead time
**e.** Don't accept a bribe from the supplier!
**f.** Place an order
**g.** Beware of overstocking!!
**h.** Write up the purchase order
**i.** Ask for a quantity discount
**j.** Make sure the supplier will respect the deadline
**k.** Purchaser or head buyer* chooses a supplier
**l.** Double-check the parts list**
**m.** Call for tender – you may need to go through a middleman
**n.** The supplier makes an offer
**o.** Ask for a quote (estimate)

*"Purchaser" is the term used in a company whereas "(head) buyer" is used in stores.
**Parts list can also be called B.O.M. (Bill of material).

## C. SOME PARTS ARE LACKING – IT'S TIME TO REORDER

*Match a phrase on the left to a phrase on the right.*

1. We have a shortage of stock. •
2. We are out of stock. •
3. We need to order more goods. •
4. We have to order the same products again. •
5. Get goods again from a supplier you can count on. •
6. If production is stopped, ask for a substitute stock. •

• **A.** Resupply from reliable supplier.
• **B.** We have missing stock.
• **C.** Request a buffer stock.
• **D.** We have run out of supplies.
• **E.** Make a repeat order.
• **F.** This is the reorder point.

## D. TRY YOUR HAND AT THESE CONFUSING WORDS

*Relax a minute! Don't forget to put the verbs in the right tense.*

**1. Briefly / shortly: a)** I shall answer your e-mail ..............., in a couple of days.
**b)** Can you tell us ............... what the situation really is?
**2. Eligible / illegible: a)** This handwritten report is totally ...............
**b)** Is he ............... to be on the works council?
**3. Look over / overlook: a)** Would you mind ............... my presentation for me?
**b)** Oh dear, they have ............... some clauses in the contract.
**4. Personal / personnel: a)** Please don't open my ............... mail.
**b)** If you're looking for a job, contact ...............

# 5 Quality

## A. THE 5 Ss

*Add the missing vowels.*

S_rt S_t in_ rder / st_re Sh_ne St_nd_rd_ze S_st_in

## B. QUALITY CATCHWORDS

*Sort the capital letters, add a suffix and find a common quality word.*

| | | | |
|---|---|---|---|
| M E O P F R R | + ance | = how well it works | = |
| A P E R A P | + ance | = what it looks like | = |
| B R L I E A | + ility | = how dependable it is | = |
| D B R A U | + ility | = how long it lasts | = |
| R B S E I E C V A | + ility | = how easy it is to use | = |
| R A C T B A E | + ility | = where it comes from | = |

## C. THE QUALITY DEPARTMENT

*Put the right word into the text.*

• Repair • Preventive action • Deviate from the norm • Non-quality cost • Meet customer requirements • Certification • Scrapped • Replace • Tolerance • Conform • Handle complaints • Goodwill • Certificate of compliance • Re-design • Testing procedures • Corrective action • Rework • Defect

One role of the quality department is to h.............. c.............. when an item is not c.............. . When you find a d.............. you should take c.............. a.............. immediately, so that you continue to m.............. c.............. r.............. and obtain a c.............. o.............. c.............. You can either r.............., r.............., r.............. or r.............. the items.
The goods which d.............. f.............. t.............. n.............. will have to be s.............. You may have to improve your t.............. p.............. or alter the t..............
Remember, p.............. a.............. will avoid n.............. q.............. c.............. and enable keeping customer g.............. Of course, we are also responsible for .........................., such as ISO.

## D. ZERO DEFECT?!

*Unscramble the letters and match them up with one of the non-quality words.*

**Snahegirk** ...................... : Wear & tear
**Salspdah** ...................... : Shoddy
**Spoisdhl** ......................: Slapdash
**Sudadtnrsab** ...................... : Unreliable

**Bda mohnkpasiwr** ...................... : Shrinkage
**Sdhoyd** ...................... : Slipshod
**Urbaleienl** ...................... : Substandard
**Wera & eatr** ...................... : Bad workmanship

# 6 Research, Development & Industrialization

## A. ADVANCED TECHNOLOGY

*For each box, match the word(s) with a definition in the opposite box.*

| | |
|---|---|
| Technological awareness | Knowing how to do something |
| Technological lead | Being rather behind in technology |
| Technological know-how | Being a technological forerunner |
| Technological gap | Keeping up to date with the latest technology |

| | |
|---|---|
| Leading-edge technology | The rapid development of new technology |
| Outdated technology | Technology which is no longer applicable |
| Obsolete technology | The latest advancement in a certain technology |
| High-tech | Old-fashioned technology |
| Rise of new technologies | The foremost position in a trend or technology |

→

→

| | |
|---|---|
| Experiment | Waiting to be protected by government authorisation |
| Breakthrough | A test under controlled conditions |
| Patent | To begin or introduce something new |
| Patent pending | A major achievement in technology which enables further progress |
| Innovate | Government authorisation to an inventor for the sole use of the invention for a set time |

| | |
|---|---|
| Design lead time | Where storage, waste and errors are kept to a minimum |
| Lean manufacturing | Calculating the cost of a given unit of a product |
| Unit costing | The time between the initiation and the completion of a design process |

| | |
|---|---|
| Pilot study | An example |
| Prototype | A preliminary study |
| Sample | An original, full-scale and working model of a new product |

## B. NEW TECHNOLOGY BUZZWORDS

↘ ***Choose the right word out of the three choices.***

**1.** The manipulation of individual atoms and molecules (e.g. for high performance tennis rackets!).
**a)** Atomtechnology **b)** Moleculology **c)** Nanotechnology
**2.** A very thin fibre made of glass, particularly used in bundles for transmitting images.
**a)** Glass fibre **b)** Optical fibre **c)** Bundle fibre
**3.** The transmission of television or radio programs which the end user receives via a dish.
**a)** Dish broadcasting **b)** Satellite broadcasting **c)** Transmission broadcasting
**4.** RFID (e.g. automatic tollbooths where you don't have to stop).
**a)** Radio for identification **b)** Radio for impatient drivers **c)** Radio frequency identification
**5.** Identification using a person's unique features (for now fingerprint, voice, iris or face).
**a)** Biometric identification **b)** Body identification **c)** Individual identification
**6.** A tiny piece of silicon with an electronic circuit (e.g. for smart cards and motherboards).
**a)** A flea **b)** A chip **c)** A ship

## C. EQUIPMENT FOR THE LAB

↘ ***Link the word in the list to the reason below.***

**1.** Apparel dispenser
**2.** Glove dispensers
**3.** Eye goggles
**4.** Laboratory bench
**5.** Cabinets
**6.** Chemical cabinets
**7.** Fume hoods
**8.** Emergency sprinklers
**9.** Stools
**10.** Scales
**11.** Microscope
**12.** Test tube (with stopper) and test tube holder
**13.** Thermometer
**14.** Heating and cooling equipment

From: The General Manager

To: The Head Lab Technician

Cc:

Subject: Our demanding new customer wants a cleanroom

In view of new customer requirements, we have to expand our facilities and upgrade our laboratory equipment. Could you please make sure that before their visit on 14th July, we have the following equipment. I have indicated the reasons for each item on the list below.

Could you also please check the efficient functioning of the following equipment?

The ultrasonic bath

The bench-top centrifuge

The environmental chamber

All the mixers, stirrers and shakers

The pumps and the valves

Thank you, and please get back to me before the end of the week to confirm all this is possible.

**a.** Better than chairs because there is no back for things to get caught on. ...

**b.** We must have new "hazard resistant" long tables conform with standards. ...

**c.** We need more accurate temperature measuring equipment. ...

**d.** From now on, specialised containers for clean clothing for "clean lab" environments are compulsory. ...

**e.** We need to be able to magnify smaller and smaller objects. ...

**f.** To hold and distribute protective gloves. ...

**g.** To warm up or cool down products during experimentation. ...

**h.** These can be activated in case of fire or chemical spillage. ...

**i.** To prevent hazardous products from getting into technicians' eyes. ...

**j.** We need these with mini hoods for accurate weighing. ...

**k.** To vent the air around experiments. ...

**l.** New stocks required of these clear cylindrical glass tubes. ...

**m.** With special safeguards for the storage of hazardous materials. ...

**n.** For general storage in compliance with 5S. ...

## D. HORRENDOUS HOMONYMS

***Oh no – not more!***

**1. Eight / ate: a)** There are .............. cakes on the plate. **b)** They ............... a lot of cakes.

**2. Board / bored: a)** She's going to .............. at school next year.

**b)** She's going to be ............. at school next year.

**3. Forward / foreword: a)** The .............. was written by a famed actor.

**b)** We're looking ............. to meeting you.

**4. Hear / here: a)** Can you .............. me? **b)** I'm over ...............

**5. Meet / meat: a)** I'd like you to eat some .............. **b)** I'd like you to ............ my greatest friend.

**6. Piece / peace: a)** I'd like to give you a .............. of my mind!

**b)** .............. and quiet, that's all he wants.

## E. BOOKWORM SPECIFICATIONS

*Answer the questions.*

### THE BOOKWORM

You love books? You want to take your book anywhere and everywhere? Just slip our lightweight "Bookworm" into your handbag or briefcase and you can bury yourself in fiction or non-fiction at will.
The "Bookworm" can even be personalized – special colours and other options.

Technical Specifications:

| THE BOOKWORM | Compare with just one (standard) book! |
|---|---|
| Length: 210 mm | Height: 240 mm |
| Width: 180 mm | Width: 145 mm |
| Depth: 12 mm | Thickness: 25 mm |
| Weight: 0.65kg | Weight: 359 g!! |

9.7" LED Display which you can adjust to suit your eyesight.
Touchpad – (with fingerprint-resistant coating)
WIFI to download your books
Built-in rechargeable battery + Multi-plug adapter

All packed in special box which can then be used as a handy "bookworm case"
H: 245 x W: 182 x D: 14 mm

For accessories, please see our website: www.bookworm.com

**1.** How high is the "Bookworm"? It's __________ high. / The height is __________
**2.** How wide is the "Bookworm"? It's __________ wide. / The width is __________
**3.** How deep is the "Bookworm"? It's __________ deep. / The depth is __________
**4.** How heavy is the "Bookworm"? It weighs __________ / The weight is __________
**5.** How long is the book? It's __________ long. / The length is __________
**6.** How thick is the book? It's __________ thick. / The thickness is __________
**7.** How much does the book weigh? It weighs __________. / The weight is __________
**8.** What are the dimensions of the "Bookworm"? __________ by __________ by__________
**9.** What is the surface area of the book? It's __________ square metres ($m^2$)
**10.** What is the cubic capacity of the box? It's __________ cubic metres ($m^3$)

NB: High = tall for a building or person; Wide = broad; Specifications = Specs; Cubic capacity = volume. You could also ask "How much can it carry?"

# 7 Sales & After Sales

## A. THE RETAIL TRADE or WHERE CAN YOU SELL IT?

↘ *Find 20 different places to sell your goods in the word snake below.*

Marketplacedepartmentstorefactoryoutletvendingmachinebulkoutlet
offlabelstoresupermarketsuperstoreonepricestoreconveniencestore
chainstoreauctionshoppingarcade/centre/mallmailorderbusinessthein
ternetofflicenceretailoutletcash&carryselfservicestore

..........................................................................................................................................

..........................................................................................................................................

..........................................................................................................................................

## B. WHAT DO YOU FIND IN THE SHOP?

↘ *Pair up the right and left columns to make a word and then match it to one of the definitions. E.g. Cas hier = cashier = 5*

| | |
|---|---|
| Cas | seller |
| Shelf | man |
| Trades | filler |
| Shop | hier |
| Sales | lifter |
| Floor / shop | person |
| Re | walker |
| Price | rate goods |
| Display | ving |
| Shel | goods |
| Second- | tag |
| Second-hand | register |
| Rec | and fittings |
| Check | out |
| Cash | eipt |
| Fixtures | unit |

**The people in the store**

**1.** Someone who sells you goods
**2.** Someone who directs customers, supervises sales...
**3.** Someone who buys things cheap and sells them at quite a profit
**4.** Someone engaged in a retail trade (or a craftsman)
**5.** Someone responsible for receiving payment for goods
**6.** Someone who puts the goods on the shelves
**7.** Someone who steals merchandise while they pretend to shop

**The things in the store**

**8.** Something used to fitout the store to display goods
**9.** Something used to calculate the amount of a transaction
**10.** Something given when you pay for goods
**11.** Something attached to an item for sale to show the price
**12.** Something which has been used before
**13.** Something for showing the goods
**14.** Something which is not first-rate, of low quality
**15.** Something horizontal, used for putting the goods on
**16.** Something you record, pay and pack your goods at

## C. TRADING TIMES

↘ *Make pairs from the list below. E.g. Niche market – Mass market.*

• Niche market • Planned purchase • Early closing hours • Retail • Weekday trading hours • Returned goods • Stock clearance sale • Refund request • Wholesale • Closing down sale • Late night opening • Mass market • Sunday trading • Impulse buying

..........................................................................................................................................

..........................................................................................................................................

..........................................................................................................................................

## D. TRADING TRENDS

***Match the question to the answer.***

| | |
|---|---|
| **a)** Seasonal swings • | • **1.** What is the main aim of your sales policy? |
| **b)** Consumer satisfaction • | • **2.** Why do you think the new computer sold so badly? |
| **c)** Market glut • | • **3.** What is that huge pile of boxes over there? |
| **d)** Tough competition • | • **4.** Why are sales so high in the summer and low in the winter? |
| **e)** Recalled defective goods • | • **5.** Why have you withdrawn that item – is there an oversupply? |

## E. PRICING and PAYMENT

***Put the right word in the sentence.***

• Instalment plan • Price cut • Charge account • List price • Grant a discount • Tax-inclusive price • Interest-free credit • Knock-down

**1.** In American stores, the ____________ is not marked on the label, so tax is added at the check-out.
**2.** The goods were a bit shop-soiled, so I asked the shop assistant if she could ________________ .
**3.** The ___________________ or RRP (Recommended Retail Price) is the price recommended by the manufacturer.
**4.** It's time for the sales in our town, there are lots of ___________________ prices – you can pick up some real bargains.
**5.** The *Business Times* have announced that there will be a 39% iron ore ___________________as from September.
**6.** With _________________ you can buy now and pay over 6 months, without paying anything extra.
**7.** However, with an ___________________ you have to negotiate the interest rate, which can vary from 0.5% to anything like 12.5%!
**8.** If you are a regular customer with a good credit history, you can open a ___________________ .

## F. CORPORATE CUSTOMERS

***Fit the right word into the gap***

| | | | |
|---|---|---|---|
| Trade secret | Trade magazines | Prospective customers | Trademarks |
| Faulty goods | Trade fair | Transactions | Supplier |
| Proposals | Put in a tender | Trade discount | Complaints |

I was looking for a **(1)** S__ __ __ __ __ __ __ _. The first thing I did was to look through the **(2)** T__ __ __ __ __ __ __ __ __ __ __ __ __ __ and then I went to the **(3)** T__ __ __ __ __ F__ __ __ __ in London to see what was on offer. I found just what I wanted. Two different **(4)** T__ __ __ __ __ __ __ __, and suggested they **(5)** P__ __ __ __ I__ __ __ __ a T__ __ __ __ . I asked them to explain their manufacturing process, but they said it was a **(6)** T__ __ __ __ __ S__ __ __ __ __ __ . Another important factor was the number of **(7)** C__ __ __ __ __ __ __ __ __ __ __ for **(8)** F__ __ __ __ __ G__ __ __ __ __ __ they averaged on a yearly basis. Times are hard, and everyone was looking for **(9)** P__________C_____________, so I reckoned I would be able to negotiate a **(10)** T__________ D__ __ __ __ __ __ __ . A few days later I got both **(11)** P__ __ __ __ __ __ __ __ __ __, chose the best one and began our business **(12)** T__ __ __ __ __ __ __ __ __ __ __ __.

## G. RECEIPTS & INVOICES

*Answer the questions below.*

**A. Mighty Munch House - NYC**

| | |
|---|---|
| 1 Cheeseburger | $20.00 |
| 1 Veggieburger | $23.00 |
| 1 Soda | $ 2.00 |
| 1 Soda | $ 2.00 |
| 1 Supersalad | $30.00 |
| 1 Salmonsalad | $30.00 |
| 1 Mega-ice | $19.00 |
| 1 Maxi-ice | $19.00 |
| 1 Cocktail | $18.00 |
| 1/2 Champagne | $24.00 |
| | 187.00 |
| Sales tax | 13.09 |
| Sub total | $200.09 |
| Gratuity | 33.66 |
| TOTAL | $233.75 |

Time: 14:33 2 customers
THANK YOU FOR YOUR PATRONAGE

**B. S.......... I............No.21**

From: Red Robin Ltd VAT Reg No. 822 192 464
Snow Street, Penhaven
To: Crocus Capers Landscape Gardening
Springwellcome Road, Somerset

Sale: Time of supply 15/02/-- Date of issue: 18/02/--

| Qty | Description & Price | Amount Excl. VAT | VAT Rate | VAT Net |
|---|---|---|---|---|
| 6 | Red roses@£25.20 | £151.20 | | |
| 4 | Yew trees @£23.60 | £ 94.40 | | |
| 6 | Holly bushes@£15.55 | £ 93.30 | 17% | £56.34 |
| | | £338.90 | | |
| Delivery | | £ 9.00 | 17% | £1.57 |
| | | £347.90 | | £57.91 |
| VAT | | £ 57.91 | | |
| TOTAL | | £405.81 | | |

Terms: Cash discount of 10% if paid within 30 days

**C. Trendy togs - Canada**

| Store | Reg | Trans | Date / time | Cashier |
|---|---|---|---|---|
| 25 | 2 | 42821 | 12/02/-- 10:21 | 83491 |

| | | |
|---|---|---|
| 77465 | Sweatshirt | $ 39.50 |
| 88390 | T-shirt | $ 15.90 |
| 85747 | Jeans | $ 39.50 |
| | SUB-TOTAL | $ 94.90 |
| GST | | $ 5.69 |
| PST | | $ 7.59 |
| TOTAL | | $108.18 |

*****************************

Card Number: 3381 3300 **** ****
Date / time: 12/02/-- 10:23
Reference: 89385821
Approved – Thank you.
Process amount to account shown.

**1.** Which is a restaurant receipt (A, B or C)?
**2.** Which is a clothing store receipt (A, B or C)?
**3.** Which is a sales invoice (A, B or C)?
**4.** What acronyms stand for Sales Tax in a) Canada b) the United Kingdom?
**5.** What is the acronym for Provincial Sales Tax?
**6.** How much is the tip?
**7.** When were the plants delivered?
**8.** When was the sales invoice made up?
**9.** How much do Crocus Capers take off the price if they pay within a month?
**10.** What is "Qty" short for?

## 1 Agriculture & Forestry

### MAKE HAY WHILE THE SUN SHINES

↘ *Put the words below into the correct box.*

• Outbuildings • Deforestation • Plow • Chainsaw • Cereal • A flock of sheep • Tractor • Barren land • Stock • Farmer • Organic • Cattle breeding • Fruit • Rodents • Drought • Poultry • Market • A tea plantation • Shed • Trailer • Sow • Vegetables • Landowner • A timber forest • Weeds • Farm labourer • A litter of pigs • Vintner • Farmhand • Combine harvester • Seafarming • Pollution • Fertilize • Farm manager • Harvest • A lumber mill • Tropical crops • Dairy • Forest ranger • Crops • Silo • Thoroughbred horses • Fell • Beekeeper • Woodcutter • Mushrooms • Farmyard • Market gardening • Season • Plant • Bad crop rotation • Vineyard • Barn

| People | Working the land | Farm machinery | Farm buildings |
|---|---|---|---|
| | | | |

| Produce | Livestock | Fieldwork for a bumper crop | Forest exploitation |
|---|---|---|---|
| | | | |

| Problems which reduce crop yield |
|---|
| |

## 2 Money & Banking

### A. A FEW FINANCIAL ANTONYMS

↘ ***Look at the word and the definition then find the antonym in the list below.***

- Bankrupt
- Loss
- Priceless
- Deflation
- Overcharged
- Mark-up
- Borrow
- In the black
- Withdraw
- Net
- Spend
- Expenditure

**1.** Lend = Give temporarily ≠ ................................................
**2.** Inflation = Rising prices ≠ ................................................
**3.** Discount = A deduction from a price ≠ ................................................
**4.** Income = Money coming in ≠ ................................................
**5.** Solvent = Able to meet your debts ≠ ................................................
**6.** Deposit = Put money into the bank ≠ ................................................
**7.** In the red = To be overdrawn ≠ ................................................
**8.** Profit = Make money from investment or business activity ≠ ................................................
**9.** Gross = Before any deductions ≠ ................................................
**10.** Undercharged = Not charged enough ≠ ................................................
**11.** Save = Economise ≠ ................................................
**12.** Worthless = Of absolutely no practical value ≠ ................................................

### B. A VISIT TO COUNTINGHOUSE COFFER BANK

↘ ***Read the story and put the appropriate word in the gap.***

- Savings account
- Maturity date
- Counterfoil / stub
- Bank statement
- Foreign currency
- ATM
- Teller
- Branch manager
- Mortgage repayment
- Exchange rate
- Home banking
- Current account
- Coins and notes
- Cheque / check book
- PIN

Yesterday, I went to see the (**1.** *Person who runs the branch of the bank*) ............................ at my local bank. I had received a (**2.** *Printed document giving the state of my account*) ............................ telling me I had an overdraft on my (**3.** *The account I use regularly*) ............................ – in other words my bank balance was negative – and that I was going to pay high interest. When I arrived the manager was busy, so I spoke to the (**4.** *person who works behind the counter*) ............................ who told me that I had money in my (**5.** *Account to save money*) ............................ so I should make a transfer. →

→ I didn't want an argument so I took money out of my deposit account and put it into my current account. Then I decided to withdraw some money from the (**6.** *Cash dispenser*) .............................
I took out my bank card, but of course I had forgotten my (**7.** *Personal Identification Number*) ............................. so it didn't work. As I was at the bank, I decided to cash a cheque instead. Oh dear – where had I put my (**8.** *Book with detachable blank cheques*) .............................? Of course, at the bottom of my handbag! So I wrote out a cheque and filled in the (**9.** *Part of the cheque to keep as a record*) ............................., and handed it over to the teller.
He gave me the money in (**10.** *Metal pieces and bits of paper representing money*) .............................
I also had some money in a (**11.** *Foreign exchange*) ............................. to deposit on my account. I asked the teller what the (**12.** *The rate of exchanging from one currency to another*) ............................. was. "Not very good, I'm afraid," he said. That didn't surprise me - up until then, it hadn't been my lucky day!
Then I waited to see the manager – I needed to ask for two things: I wanted to take out a (**13.** *Credit for buying property*) ............................. to buy a new house, and I needed a (**14.** *Credit for personal purchases*) ............................. to pay for my son's wedding.
But luck can change.... After lengthy discussions, the manager agreed to both my requests. The (**15.** *The monthly payment to payback money borrowed*) ............................. for the house would be over 10 years. He told me that I had invested some money and that the (**16.** *The date by which the obligation had to be repaid*) ............................. was next month - now that was good news!
Finally, he asked if I had a computer and an Internet connection. I gave a positive answer so he politely suggested that I try (**17.** *Banking through the Internet*) .............................!

## C. UMPTEEN CONFUSING WORDS

↘ ***Choose between the two words to complete the sentences below.***

**1. Alone / lonely:**
**a)** She would much rather work ...............
**b)** Being right at the top can be very ...............
**2. As far as / until:**
**a)**They won't be here ............... 7pm.
**b)** Take the Phoenix road ............... the roundabout.
**3. Audience / spectators:**
**a)** The ............... clapped loudly at the end of the play.
**b)** The number of ............... at the match was amazing.
**4. Most / the most:**
**a)** ............... people are still wary of fringe medicine.
**b)** ............... important thing is to be on time for an interview.
**5. Homework / housework:**
**a)** The teacher has given us too much ...............
**b)** Do you have a daily to do the ...............?

**6. Invaluable / valueless:**

**a)** That is no good at all. It's ...............

**b)** Please be careful with that painting, it's...............

**7. Game / play:**

**a)** We had a good ............... of tennis.

**b)** Do you ............... chess?

**8. Journey / travel (x2) / trip / voyage:**

**a)** Sorry, Mr Smith is on a business ...............

**b)** He prefers air ................(nom) He likes to ............. (verbe) by sea.

**c)** The settlers were excited about their ............. to the Far West.

**d)** The ............... across the Atlantic was just amazing.

## D. AN INVESTMENT ON THE STOCK MARKET

↘ *Read the newspaper articles and choose the right title.*

- A BULL MARKET AT LAST
- INSIDER DEALING REVEALED
- THE COMMODITY MARKET
- INVEST IN BLUE-CHIP COMPANIES

**1.**____________________

Jobbers and even stockbrokers came out on strike today following a government announcement that the director of the huge XBZ company had sold all his stocks and shares, having been forewarned by financial consultants that things were going badly and that there would be a downturn in the face value of the shares. "A politician would never behave like that," said a government spokesman.

**2.**____________________

Given the current bear market, where prices are falling fast, the safest investment is in gilts (or gilt-edged securities). If you want to gamble on the stock exchange, you may get a lower return on investment on settlement day, but at least it's a safer bet.

**3.**____________________

No one was more surprised than the significant fund-management companies when there was a sudden upturn in share prices at the end of the week. On average, shares closed at 5% up compared with their opening price. "We should see some decent dividends at last," was the hopeful remark of one shareholder.

**4.**____________________

Why not try your luck in coffee or tea rather than stocks or bonds? Scale down your investments on the stock exchange and speculate on the futures of raw and primary products. Find out more about the regulated commodity exchanges on www.letmeinvest.com.

## E. ACRONYMS (WHAT DOES IT STAND FOR?)

↘ *Match the acronym to what it stands for.*
*Tip: Learn the alphabet by groups of sounds rather than in alphabetical order!*

| | |
|---|---|
| APR • | • Enterprise Requirement Planning |
| ASAP • | • Computer-Assisted Design and Manufacturing |
| ATM • | • Plan, Do, Check, Act |
| BSI • | • Exchange Rate Mechanism |
| CADM • | • British Standards Institute |
| CEO • | • Year-to-date |
| CPI • | • Value Added Tax |
| DDD • | • Stock-Keeping Unit |
| ERP • | • Point Of Sale |
| FAI • | • Annualized Percentage Rate |
| ERM • | • Consumer Price Index |
| FYI • | • Stamped Addressed Envelope |
| NCV • | • For Your Information |
| PDCA • | • First Article Inspection |
| POS • | • As Soon As Possible |
| PTO • | • Deadline Delivery Date |
| OEM • | • Please Turn Over |
| VAT • | • World Wide Web |
| S.A.E • | • Chief Executive Officer |
| SKU • | • Automatic Teller Machine |
| WWW • | • Frequently Asked Questions |
| YTD • | • Original Equipment Manufacturer |
| OTC • | • Return On Investment |
| ROI • | • Over The Counter |
| OTD • | • No Commercial Value |
| FAQ • | • On-Time Delivery |

# 3 Insurance

## A. HAVE YOU GOT INSURANCE COVERAGE ?

↘ *Complete the insurance mind-mapping.*

• Settlement for the claim • Act of vandalism • Life assurance • Annuity • To be insured • Insure baggage against loss • Marine insurance • Annuity policy • Full coverage • Fair wear and tear • All risks policy • Comprehensive • To underwrite • Damage • Insurance policy • Casualty insurance • Assess value • Car insurance • Act of God • To be covered by insurance • Annual Insurance premium • Life insurance • Third party fire and theft • Annuity due • Injured party • Burglary insurance • Assess damage • Underwriter • Certificate of insurance • Health insurance

DIFFERENT KINDS OF INSURANCE

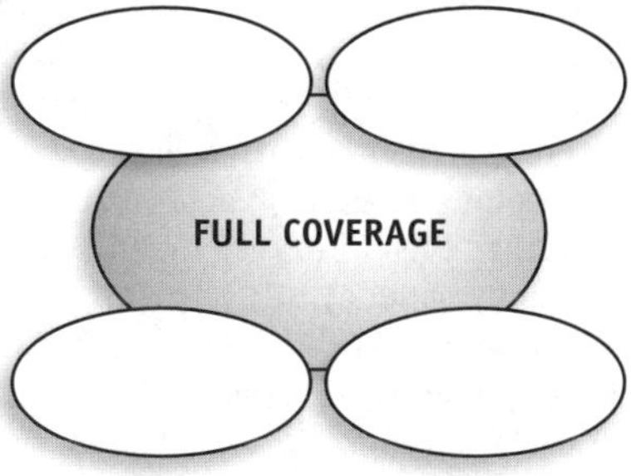
FULL COVERAGE

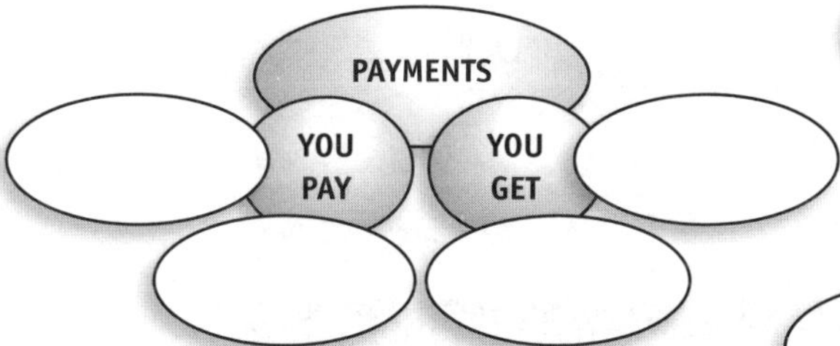
PAYMENTS
YOU PAY
YOU GET

TAKING OUT INSURANCE

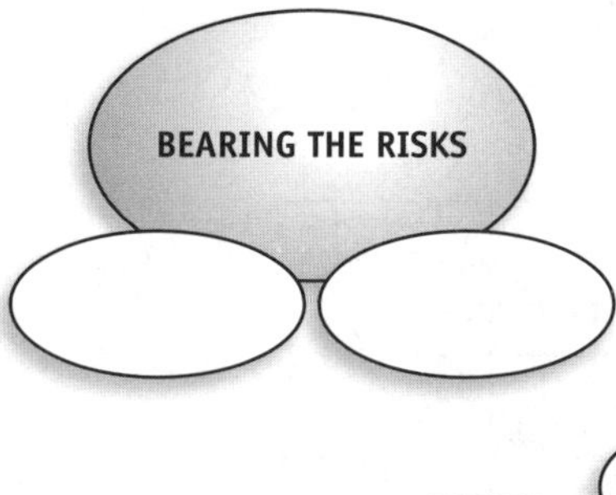
BEARING THE RISKS

PUT IN A CLAIM

## B. COUNTLESS CONFUSING WORDS

↘ *Choose between the two words to complete a) and b). If necessary, put the verb in the right tense.*

**1. Lend / Borrow: a)** He had to ............... money from the bank.
**b)** Can you ............... me your mobile a minute?
**2. Pour / Spill: a)** I'm so sorry, I've ............... wine all over the tablecloth!
**b)** It's good wine, so ............... it slowly into the decanter.
**3. Priceless / worthless: a)** That antique sofa table is ...............
**b)** However, that laminated cupboard is ...............
**4. Receipt / recipe: a)** Could you text me the ............... for that delicious cake?
**b)** Bother, I forgot to keep the ............... for this shirt.
**5. Right / good: a)** He's very .............. at maths.
**b)** I hope you get the ................ answer to the question.
**6. Say / tell: a)** What time is it? ............... Jo to hurry up, will you?
**b)** Could you ............... to Tom that the film begins at 9?

# 4 Land Settlement & Zoning Regulations

## A. URBAN PLANNING & WHO IS INVOLVED

↘ *Answer the clues to complete the word puzzle. N.B. For "Business", please write "BUS".*

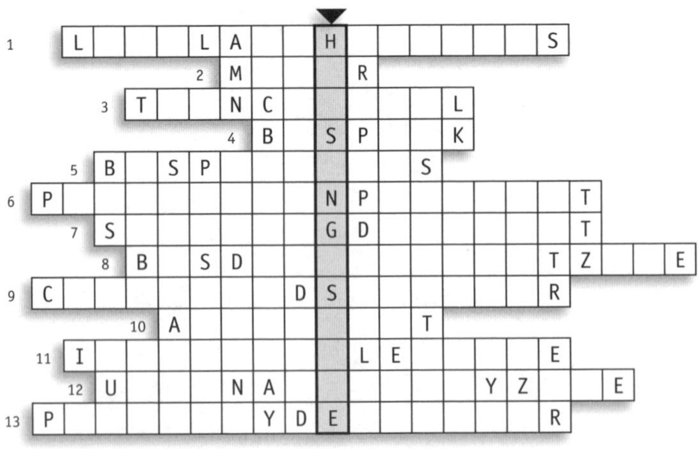

**1.** The local government body
**2.** The influential head of 1. in a town, city or municipal corporation
**3.** Another word for municipal corporation
**4.** An area where many office buildings are grouped together
**5.** The land and buildings of a business
**6.** An area where cars are prohibited
**7.** An area with lots of shops
**8.** An area where businesses are to be developed
**9.** A person who officially surveys land
**10.** The person who does the designs
**11.** An industrial area
**12.** A town area of mixed industrial and commercial businesses.
**13.** Someone who develops property
**Down:** An area of housing

## B. LET'S DO SOME TOWN PLANNING

↘ ***What is the question for the following answers?***

**1.** Government aid
**2.** Planning permission
**3.** Detailed description and blueprint
**4.** Public transport system
**5.** Labour market area
**6.** Catchment area
**7.** The land register
**8.** Building ground
**9.** Reclaim land

**A.** What about choosing a local area of at least 10 hectares where there are jobs and a workforce?

**B.** Couldn't we put to use that damp waste land?

**C.** How about commuters? What do we plan for them?

**D.** Why don't we ask for help from the government?

**E.** Might I suggest we officially record our ownership of the land?

**F.** Shouldn't we get authorization to build?

**G.** Would you like me to look for land to build on?

**H.** Don't you think we need information from the architect?

**I.** What if we work out what area depends on the local town (e.g. for schools and public services)?

# 5 Legal Matters

## A LITTLE BIT OF LEGAL JARGON

↘ ***Choose the right answer. (There could be 1 or 2 right answers.)***

**1.** The late Mr. Smith died without leaving a will – in other words ....................
**a)** Intestate **b)** Inherit **c)** Intact

**2.** He was so surprised, he .................... a fortune!
**a)** Herited **b)** Inherited **c)** Heir

→

→ **3.** The .................... was proven to be the guilty party.
**a)** Victims **b)** Culprit **c)** Offender

**4.** He was .................... for murder.
**a)** Proscribed **b)** Persecuted **c)** Prosecuted

**5.** The lawyer provided .................... of corruption.
**a)** Poof **b)** Evidence **c)** Proof

**6.** The .................... was asked to testify because he had seen the accident.
**a)** Witness **b)** Testimony **c)** Testifier

**7.** The accused pleaded .................... to the gun charge – he didn't have a gun!
**a)** Innocent **b)** Not guilty **c)** Not coupable

**8.** If you find it hard to pay your attorney, you can ask for ....................
**a)** Legal assistance **b)** Legal aid **c)** Lawyer aid

**9.** He wouldn't pay his fine so they had to call in the .................... to collect the money.
**a)** Money collector **b)** Bailiff **c)** Bailer

**10.** A lawyer, who has passed the bar exam, can be either a ....................
**a)** Solicitor / barman **b)** Avocado / barrister **c)** Solicitor / barrister

**11.** The plaintiff instituted proceedings against the ....................
**a)** Accused **b)** Crook **c)** Defendant

**12.** The journalist was ................ for libel.
**a)** Sued **b)** Suited against **c)** Sooed

**13.** The unfairly sacked employee took the case to the Employment ..................
**a)** Tribune **b)** Tribunal **c)** Tribunial

**14.** Stealing chewing gum from the local store was considered a ....................
**a)** Pretty offence **b)** Pity offence **c)** Petty offence

**15.** He put on too much weight, and brought ...................... against the chocolate company.
**a)** Civilian action **b)** Civil action **c)** A lawsuit

**16.** I would like to ................... charges against my supplier.
**a)** File **b)** Fill **c)** Put

# 6 The Media - Press and Publishing, Television and Radio

## A. THE PRINTED WORD

*Sort out the mixed-up words in the following articles / e-mails. The first letter is done for you.*

- Page rate
- Readership
- Editor
- Going to press
- Circulation
- Royalties
- Headlines
- Coverage
- Proofreaders
- Features
- Printing works
- Copyright
- Subscription
- Daily
- Newsletter
- Print run
- Complimentary copy
- Renewal
- Freelance
- Press Clipping

**NEWS IN BRIEF**

**1.** Ctrnaouicil .................. of the new newspaper *"Latest Update"* has reached record numbers. **2.** Rapriesehd ................ has outstripped other **3.** dliya ................ newspapers. It must be said that the **4.** cegveroa ................ of current events is outstanding and the **5.** feuetsra ................ always break the news about topics of interest.

To: All **6.** Flceearne ................ journalists From: The Editor's Assistant
The **7.** eoirdt ................ would like all self-employed journalists to note that their expenses are to be submitted before the last Friday of each month, and will be paid within 2 weeks.

It'll be in the **8.** hieanlsed ............ tomorrow! Mr. Busybody is to be taken to court for infringement of **9.** chpgroity .................. It would appear that over 50% of his book contains articles which have already been published.
John – Could you send a **10.** cnpaetilmrmyo cypo................ of the new trade magazine right away to BLB Inc? They would like to take out a **11.** socnibitsrpu ................ and also want to be informed about the **12.** pgea rtae ................ for advertising. Just a little reminder - their subscription to *"Friendly Finances"* is also due for **13.** raelnwe .................

**IN-HOUSE JOURNAL**

Could anyone who has an interesting column, editorial or **14.** psesr cipignpl ................ to put in the **15.** neletwrets ................ please give it to the works council before next Friday?
Thank you very much in advance.

To all editors and **16.** poforrasedre ................
Publication of *"How to wine and dine healthily"*.
We are **17.** gngio to psesr ................ in 2 weeks, time. The 18. pgninitr wsrko ................ have been informed that we have decided on a **19.** ptnirrnu ................ of 5,000 copies to begin with. The author is still negotiating his **20.** rysteoila ................ – he reckons that a publishing house such as ours should be able to offer more for the publishing rights to his book.

## B. HERE WE GO AGAIN! - HOMONYMS

*Choose between the two words to complete a) and b).*

**1. Patience / patients**
a) That doctor has got a lot of very sick ...............
b) He's very ............... with them all.

**2. Weak / week**
a) That's his ............... point I'm afraid.
b) That's the ............... gone by already!

**3. Which / Witch**
a) The ............... mixed the brew in the cauldron.
b) ............... one do you prefer?

**4. Where / wear**
a) What shall I ............... to the prom?
b) ............... is the party going to be held?

**5. Weather / whether**
a) The ............... will probably be lovely tomorrow.
b) I don't know ............... to go to the cinema or not.

**6. Would / wood**
a) ............... you like a cup of tea?
b) Try to buy sustainable ............... products.

## C. TELEVISION & RADIO

*Put the words in the list into the right column. Then complete the sentences on the next page.*

- Serial
- Weather forecast
- Remote control
- News
- Cable TV
- Current affairs program
- Turn on / off
- Soap opera
- Turn up
- DVD player
- Sports program
- Host
- Censor
- Quiz show
- Satellite TV
- Commercial
- Variety show
- TV cartoon
- Viewer
- AM / FM radio
- Thriller
- Documentary
- Turn over
- Broadcaster
- Sitcom
- Guest
- Chat / talk show
- News reader / anchor
- Game show
- Couch potato
- Reality show
- Turn down
- Turn over / change channel

| Programs | Equipment | Verbs | People |
|---|---|---|---|
| | | | |

**1.** Live coverage of the Winter Olympics can be seen on the ____________________ .
**2.** It's best to put the ____________________ on at prime time – for the biggest consumer audience.
**3.** The ____________________ didn't realize the news wasn't finished – he was still on the air when he started chatting to his colleague.
**4.** The ____________________ was recorded off screen to be sure of no cheating about the answers.
**5.** Broadcasting has become much easier with the development of ____________________ TV and ____________________ TV.
**6.** The television network is pleased with their viewership results – that is the number of ____________________ .
**7.** I always ____________________ the TV when the program is finished on channel 14.
**8.** "My favourite program on their radio station is the one which talks about what is going on at the moment ." "Oh, you mean the ____________________".

## 7 Real Estate & Corporate Property

### A. ACCOMMODATION with or without a garden / yard

***Match the word to the definition.***

**a)** Bungalow **b)** Housing estate **c)** Flatlet / studio / bedsit **d)** Semi-detached **e)** Houseboat **f)** Turnkey factory **g)** Cottage **h)** Mobile home **i)** Tower block **j)** Caravan **k)** Detached / single family homes **e)** Office block **f)** Skyscraper **g)** Flat / apartment **h)** Terraced / row houses (party wall)

**1.** A house standing alone ..........
**2.** A house joined to another one ..........
**3.** Several houses joined together ..........
**4.** A small house (usually with two floors and often with character) ..........
**5.** A house on one floor only ..........
**6.** A house you tow along behind your car ..........
**7.** A house which can be moved around by a lorry ..........
**8.** A house on the water ..........
**9.** An area where there are several houses (which often look alike) ..........
**10.** A set of rooms on one floor for residential use ..........
**11.** A very tall apartment building ..........
**12.** A tall building for business purposes ..........
**13.** An industrial building ready-for-use ..........
**14.** A studio ..........
**15.** A building of exceptional height which towers over everything else ..........

## B. INSIDE THE HOUSE

***Match the word to the description.***

Attic
Basement / cellar
Bathroom
Garage
Landing
Spare room / guest room
Staircase
Hall / hallway
Kitchen
Living / family / sitting room
Bedroom
Office / study

**1.** Somewhere to do some work ..........................................
**2.** Here you go up and down ..........................................
**3.** It's under the house (for storing wine?!) ..............................
**4.** Time for some cooking ..........................................
**5.** Shower, bathtub ..........................................
**6.** Let's go to sleep (upstairs or downstairs) ..............................
**7.** A place for storage at the top of the house ..........................
**8.** Even the car has somewhere to go ..............................
**9.** A room for friends and relations ..............................
**10.** Sit in here to read a book, to chat, to watch TV ..................
**11.** Once you've come in the front door ..............................
**12.** An area at the top of the stairs ..............................

## C. RENTING PROPERTY

***Find the answer to the question.***

**a)** Life tenancy
**b)** Tenancy agreement
**c)** Rent
**d)** To let
**e)** Sub-lease / sublet
**f)** Office space to let

**1.** What would you put in an advertisement if you wanted someone in your offices? ........................
**2.** What is the name of the contract you sign for a rental? ..............................
**3.** What is the verb to say you pay to use someone else's premises, or the noun to say what you pay monthly? ..............................
**4.** What is it when you sign a rental contract for a very, very long time? ..............................
**5.** What is the verb which describes allowing the use of rooms in return for payment? ......................
**6.** Is this one legal? To let a room which you hold by lease to another tenant? ..............................

## D. PURCHASING PROPERTY

***Complete the story on the next page.***

- Particulars of sale
- Housewarming party
- Provisional sales agreement
- Gazumped
- Estate agent / realtor
- Time share property
- Property deed
- Plot / patch
- Estate agency
- Restricted or unrestricted access
- Leasehold
- Survey
- Ownership
- Freehold

I was looking for a property to buy, so I went to see an **(1)** .................. ................... where I met the **(2)** ................. ....................., who took me around the neighbourhood to visit several houses, manor houses and stately homes. I asked for the **(3)** .................... .................. ................ and for further information, for example, the size of the **(4)**...................... if the property was for sale **(5)** ............................. or **(6)** ........................... , and if there were **(7)** ........................... or .................................... ...................... to the estate. We had a **(8)** ............................. done to check there were going to be no surprises, and then signed the **(9)** ........................... ........................... ...................................... . We already have a **(10)** ...................... ..................... ....................... in Spain, so we wanted full **(11)** .................................. this time. We were frightened of being **(12)** ............................ (in other words, that someone else would offer a better price) but all's well that ends well - we got the **(13)** ................ ................, and a couple of weeks later moved in and had a **(14)** .................... .................... .

## E. A NEW LANDLORD

↘ *Put the words you find in the snake into the right circle.*

housingallowancehomeownersurveyorrelocatetenantdecorateneighbour estateagentremovallandlordlandowner

**PEOPLE**

**MOVING HOUSE**

## F. THE CONSTRUCTION INDUSTRY

↘ *Find the odd man out and why.*

1. foundations - roof - wall - surveyor
2. design - build - contract - architect - interior designer - landscape architect
3. civil engineer - mechanical engineer - general contractor - structural engineer - electrical engineer
4. building - heavy / highway - industrial - building site
5. concrete - wood - cost overrun - steel - stone
6. glass - zoning and building code requirements – cinder blocks – stone – brick

## G. PUBLIC UTILITIES

*Read the dialogue and the advert, and answer the true / false questions on the next page.*

**CHANGING ELECTRICITY AND GAS SUPPLIERS:**

Good morning. I would like to save money and switch my utility bills. I have some questions to ask.

Fire away.

Can I save a lot of money from switching?

Yes, of course, and switching is free.

Do I need a new meter?

No, your new supplier will use the same wires, pipes and meters as you use at the moment.

Is there a lot of paperwork involved?

No, there are just one or two forms to fill in.

What about billing?

You can still receive a paper bill if you like. Otherwise you could go for an on-line billing plan – which is cheaper for the customer and for the supplier.

How can I be sure to find a reliable supplier?

If I were you, I would ask around and check on the Internet.

What happens if I have a gas leak or a power cut after changing supplier?

No problem, we have a 24-hour emergency help line. Just call 0800 616 616.

DON'T FORGET TO ASK FOR A METER READING BEFORE YOU CHANGE!

**Consumer Advice Column**

HOW TO SAVE MONEY ON YOUR WATER BILL

Use a full dishwasher rather than washing up by hand.

Install a low-flow shower head.

Take shorter showers – and don't take a bath!

Don't let the water run while you brush your teeth.

Check regularly for leaks or dripping taps.

Collect rain water in barrels to water the garden.

**REMEMBER – EVERY CUBIC METRE IS METERED!!**

Contact the Department of Public Utilities or Water Board for more tips for reducing your water bill, or for details on how to renovate your sanitary sewer and drainage systems – or even how to heat your water using solar panels.

**True or false:**

**1.** You can't save money by changing your utility supplier.
**2.** A meter is used to measure your consumption of water, gas and electricity.
**3.** You have to download your bill off the Internet.
**4.** If you start to smell gas, you have to wait 24 hours before getting help.
**5.** When you have no electricity supply you should call an oh eight hundred number.
**6.** An electric company employee should note down the number which is on the meter before you change supplier.
**7.** Washing up by hand is better for the environment and for your pocketbook.
**8.** The ad infers that you save water if you don't take a bath.
**9.** It's better to harvest rainwater to help those vegetables and flowers grow.
**10.** You can upgrade the way you treat your waste water.

## 8 Volunteer Work

### A. LEND A HELPING HAND

↘ ***Take a word from column 1 and a word from column 2 to fill in the gaps.***

| 1. First word | 2. Second word |
|---|---|
| raise – rummage – sponsored – fund – financial – monthly – needy – charity – local – humanitarian | branch – areas – shops – donation – organisation – raiser – marathon – gain – sales – money |

**CHARITY BEGINS AT HOME**
**It's an old idiom, but it's not what we think! How can you help us?**

**1.** Work for others for no material or F____________ G____________.
**2.** Volunteer for our overseas H____________ O____________ .
**3.** Sign up for short-term assignments in N____________ A____________ if you are a qualified doctor.
**4.** Join a L____________ B____________ of "Houses for the Homeless".
**5.** Help out in one of our local C____________ S____________ .
**6.** We need to R____________ M____________ – here are some ideas how you can help.
**7.** Donate jumble for us to sell at our annual R____________ S____________.
**8.** Become a F____________ R____________ and think up lots of new ideas.
**9.** Go on a S____________ M____________ (walk / bicycle ride / swim...).
**10.** Make a M____________ D____________(or yearly if you prefer).
Spread the word!

## 1 Letters, Faxes or E-mails

### A. A BIT OF LETTER WRITING

↘ ***Below is a list of expressions you could use on the telephone, or in a more informal e-mail. Please find the equivalent expression to be used in written communication, among the selection underlined in the letters on the following page.***

**a.** Not applicable: ..........
**b.** Best regards / kind regards (Dear Mr. Blogs): ..........
**c.** The letter which is the upshot of another letter: ..........
**d.** The post was sent to the wrong address: ..........
**e.** Following your letter: ..........
**f.** Send it on: ..........
**g.** Request for information: ..........
**h.** We confirm we have received...: ..........
**i.** The second of the two people mentioned: ..........
**j.** Please turn over (the page): ..........
**k.** Please: ..........
**l.** For: ..........
**m.** The original: ..........
**n.** In a different envelope: ..........
**o.** By the next post going out: ..........
**p.** Without waiting any longer: ..........
**q.** Without acknowledgement: ..........
**r.** Best regards / kind regards (Dear Sir): ..........
**s.** Here is...: ..........
**t.** Stamped, addressed envelope: ..........
**u.** Something to make you remember: ..........
**v.** Complete: ..........
**w.** If you need to know anything else...: ..........
**x.** We are sorry if this has been a bore: ..........
**y.** On the back of this page: ..........
**z.** Quick answer: ..........
**aa.** Let us know you get...: ..........
**bb.** Demand in writing: ..........
**cc.** An official record of postage and delivery for which you pay a supplement: ..........
**dd.** Sorry: ..........

Our ref:
Your ref:

Dear Sir or Madam
**1.** Further to your letter of 27th March, **2.** please find enclosed our price list as requested. The samples will follow **3.** under separate cover.
**4.** We would be grateful if you could **5.** acknowledge receipt of the parcel.
Should you wish to order, could you please **6.** fill in the reply coupon below.
**7.** Yours faithfully,

---

Dear Mr. Smith
**8.** We acknowledge receipt of your letter dated 14th March in which you inform us that you have not received the payment we dispatched on 20th January. The cheque was sent by **9.** registered delivery (we enclose the receipt), and the money has been withdrawn from our bank account.
We do not appreciate receiving a **10.** reminder from you for something which is an error in your own accounting department.
**11.** Yours sincerely,

---

Dear Mrs. Monkton
I am writing **12.** on behalf of my client, Mr. Jack Rivers, who is still awaiting payment of his insurance claim. His repeated letters and phone calls to you remain **13.** unacknowledged, and he has now had to ask for legal aid.
We expect a reply by **14.** return of post.

---

Dear Ms. Berry
Thank you for your **15.** inquiry about our evening classes. Please fill out the questionnaire and complete the form **16.** overleaf and return it to us, with remittance and a **17.** S.A.E. one month before you wish to start. If anything on the form does not apply to you, just put **18.** N/A in the box.
**19.** Should you require any further information, please contact the secretary.
**20.** P.T.O.

---

Dear Miss Wheeler
**21.** We would like to apologise for the late delivery of the goods you ordered 3 months ago. In fact, it was a problem of **22.** misdirected mail - the postcode you gave us was wrong, and the goods were returned to our factory.
**23.** Please accept our apologies for any inconvenience which has been caused.

---

Dear Ms. Thomson
Thank you for your **24.** prompt reply to our job offer, and we are delighted to hear that you will be joining our team in September. Could you sign the contracts enclosed and send back the **25.**top copy within a fortnight? You will then receive a **26.** follow-up letter from the H.R. department, giving you further details about company policy, etc.

---

Dear Doctor Lewis
Thank you for the letter about your patient, Henry Hypo. I am afraid I cannot prescribe the medicine you request without prior approval from a specialist. Could you send a **27.** written request to the **28.** latter, so that I can get on with treating the former within the recommended 2-month period? We should get on with this **29.** without further delay.

---

Dear Peter,
I don't know Simon's address. Could you **30.** please forward this catalogue to him?
Thanks very much in advance. Kind regards,

## B. WHAT'S IN A NAME?

*Put a tick in the right box.*

| | Full name | Surname / Family name | First name / Christian name / Forename | Middle name | Nickname |
|---|---|---|---|---|---|
| James | | | | | |
| Adam | | | | | |
| Jimbo | | | | | |
| James Adam Smith | | | | | |
| Smith | | | | | |

*Note: In English we put the first name first!!*

## C. GET THE TITLE RIGHT

*Match the title to the definition.*

**1.** Mr. • • **A.** An unmarried woman
**2.** Mrs. • • **B.** A married or single man
**3.** Miss • • **C.** A married or single woman
**4.** Ms. • • **D.** A married woman

*Remember: In English, Mr., Mrs., Miss or Ms. is always used with a surname, e.g. Mr. Smith.*

## D. SENDING AN E-MAIL

*Replace the highlighted words / symbols by one of the words underneath.*

forward: .................. UK: .......................... org: ......................... com: ........................
at: ........................... dot: ......................... spam: ....................... delete: .....................

From: Tony Broke
To: information@thebank. company
Cc: Jerry Loan
Subject: Borrowing money to set up a company

Following my request for a £100,000 loan, I would be grateful if you could send on this e-mail to your head office.
As you can see from the attachment, our business plan is certainly sound and we count on making a huge profit after only five years.
We have close links with certain non-profit organisations (such as charity.united kingdom, or helpusout.organisation who will give their backing).

Please do not erase this message. It is not an unsolicited message.

*Remember: The tone of an e-mail can be formal or informal, depending on the recipient.*

## E. WHERE DOES IT GO?

***Put the number in the right place on the sheet of paper. Does it look the same as in the answers?***

**1.** At the top
**2.** At the bottom
**3.** On the left
**4.** On the right
**5.** Top right / In the top right-hand corner
**6.** Bottom left / In the bottom left-hand corner
**7.** In the middle / centre of the page
**8.** Around the edge

# 2 Telephone

## A. THANK YOU FOR CALLING

***Match the sentence (1-14) to the thought (A-N).***

**1.** Good morning, could I speak to Neil Groover please? "Speaking".
**2.** Can we book a conference call for 3:15 this afternoon?
**3.** The person you are calling is unavailable. Could you call back later please?
**4.** (Could you) hold the line please?
**5.** I'm putting you through.
**6.** Mr. Jones on the line / I'm afraid the line is busy.
**7.** Would you like to leave a message? / Can I take a message?
**8.** Could you give me your mobile number?
**9.** I'm afraid you have dialled the wrong number.
**10.** I looked up the number in the phone book, but they must be ex-directory / an unlisted number.
**11.** It's a free-phone number so we can call for information.
**12.** Your call is in a queue, please hold.
**13.** "If you speak French, press 1, if you speak English, press 2. If you are calling about….."
**14.** Thank you for your help / It was nice speaking to you. Goodbye.

**A.** As far as I can tell, Mr. Jones is always on the telephone.
**B.** Oh good, I can call as often as I like!
**C.** I'm not sure I want to be available to that customer 24/7!
**D.** That's lucky, got him the first time!
**E.** I thought I was never going to end that call!
**F.** This is about the 4th time I've called back already.
**G.** Can you make sure he gets the message?
**H.** This could be a long wait.
**I.** Oh no, here comes the music!
**J.** I knew I needed new glasses.
**K.** Oh no, I hate speaking English when I cannot see the other people!
**L.** Perhaps if we look on the Internet we can find a contact number.
**M.** I'll never get to like voice mail.
**N.** Oh good, I'll be talking to Mr. Smith in a second.

## B. IS HE ON THE BLOWER? (= on the phone!)

***Choose the right response to the following sentences.***

**1.** Could I speak to Peter please?
**a)** I am Peter. **b)** This is Peter.

**2)** I would like to speak to Jenny please.
**a)** It's me here. **b)** Speaking.

**3.** She put the phone down in the middle of our conversation?!
**a)** She hung up on you? **b)** She dropped it?

**4.** Sorry, the line was disconnected.
**a)** Yes, we were cut off. **b)** Yes, we were cut up.

**5.** I would like to speak to Jerry Can please.
**a)** Hold on. Jerry, it's your call! **b)** Hold on. Jerry, it's for you!

**6.** Could you leave me a message, then?
**a)** Yes, I'll use your voice mail. **b)** Yes, I'll use your vocal box.

**7.** So, you'll give me a ring.
**a)** Yes, I'm engaged. **b)** Yes, I'll call you later.

**8.** Do you know Barking & Co's number?
**a)** Not off-hand, but I'll search. **b)** Not off-hand, but I'll look it up.

**9.** Shall I continue, or are you in a hurry?
**a)** Not at all, do stop. **b)** Not at all, go on.

**10.** Can you hang on a mo?
**a)** Yes, I can wait. **b)** Who is mo?

**11.** I must ring off now.
**a)** The chimes sound lovely. **b)** Well, it was nice speaking to you.

**12.** I'll give you a buzz next week.
**a)** Yes, that would be nice. **b)** Watch out for the bees.

**13.** It says "blocked caller" on my phone – I haven't blocked anyone.
**a)** They've withheld their caller I.D. **b)** The phone network is blocked.

**14.** That was a pushy phone salesman!
**a)** How nice! **b)** Did he talk you into buying a new phone?

**15.** I'll give you a bell when I know the answer to that one.
**a)** What am I going to do with a bell? **b)** That's kind, I'll look forward to it.

**16.** Did you touch base with your brother in the end?
**a)** Yes, I managed to get hold of him at last. **b)** No, it's a touch screen.

# 3 Contracts

## A. LAY DOWN THE REGULATIONS

↘ ***Read through the contract, and match the following definitions to the underlined words.***

**1.** a fee paid to retain services: ......................
**2.** to abide by the regulations: ......................
**3.** tiny writing at the bottom of a contract: ......
..................................................................
**4.** lawfully: ................................................
**5.** formalized in a letter: ...............................
**6.** formulated: ...........................................
**7.** ...... : ...................................................
**8.** responsible: ..........................................
**9.** in good faith: ........................................
**10.** compulsory: .........................................
**11.** who have signed below: ..........................
**12.** contingent on: .......................................
**13.** looked over and agreed to: .......................
**14.** except if otherwise stated: .......................
**15.** stick to: ................................................
**16.** an agreement not in writing: ....................
**17.** the actual current price: ..........................
**18.** a date before: ........................................
**19.** promise to: ...........................................
**20.** 3 copies: ..............................................

**GENERAL TERMS AND CONDITIONS OF SALE**

**Clause 1: Overview**

The General Terms and Conditions of Sale described hereinafter set forth the rights and obligations of the vendor, Luxlife, and its customer in connection with the sale of a yacht.
Any order placed with Luxlife implies that the <u>undersigned</u> has agreed to <u>abide by</u> the General Terms and Conditions of Sale.

**Clause 2: Order**

Order is final when <u>confirmed in writing</u>.

**Clause 3: Prices**

The price of the product being sold is the <u>price in effect</u> on the date on which the order is placed.

**Clause 4: Delivery**

Luxlife <u>undertakes</u> to deliver the yacht within one year following a firm order.

**Clause 5: Force majeure**

Luxlife shall not be <u>liable</u> if the yacht should sink because of an Act of God.

**Clause 6: Acceptance. Transfer of risks**

Unless otherwise agreed in writing, the risks relating to the product shall be transferred to the customer upon dispatch.

**Clause 7: Terms and conditions of payment**

<u>Unless otherwise stipulated</u>, the invoice is payable upon delivery. →

→ **Clause 8: Warranty**

The warranty shall apply to all parts of the yacht. Said warranty shall cover the repair or replacement of defective parts by Luxlife at its expense.

Should the goods delivered been damaged during transport, or should the goods not meet the requirements of the buyer, the latter retains the right to refuse delivery, subject to expressing the reason for the return on the delivery note, upon reception of the aforementioned goods. Luxlife shall be paid a retainer for the general maintenance of the yacht.

**Clause 9: Liability & damages**

Luxlife's liability shall be strictly limited to the obligations set forth above, defined in clause 8 herein.

**Clause 10: Retention of title clause**

By right, Luxlife shall retain title to the products being sold until the price – principal and ancillary costs – has been paid in full, or until such time as the goods are sold to the purchaser's customers by way of bona fide sale at the full market value. To comply with clause 7, no unwritten agreement to the contrary shall be accepted.

**Clause 11: Disputes**

Any dispute relating to the interpretation and performance hereof shall be governed by French law. If the dispute cannot be resolved out of court, it will be referred to the Commercial Court of Paris.

The contract was signed in triplicate on 20th November 20— Read and approved:
(This contract cannot be antedated) Please sign on the dotted line: ....................................
The contract is binding to both parties. Once signed, you have become party to the contract and entered into an agreement with Luxlife. Please confirm you have read the small print.

## B. UNDERSTANDING THE AGREEMENT

↘ *Find a synonym for the following words – the answer lies in the preposition (except 3 & 10).*

| | | | |
|---|---|---|---|
| 1 | Aforementioned | A | Concerning this – of this agreement |
| 2 | Undermentioned | B | After this date or as from now on |
| 3 | Entitlement | C | With this |
| 4 | Hereafter | D | In this contract |
| 5 | Hereby | E | Right |
| 6 | Herein | F | To this document |
| 7 | Hereof | G | I stated before |
| 8 | Hereto | H | Nevertheless |
| 9 | Herewith | I | Stated below (also: hereunder,hereinafter) |
| 10 | Notwithstanding | J | By means of this act |

## C. THE BEGINNING, THE MIDDLE AND THE END OF THE CONTRACT

↘ *Add vowels to find the words.*

1. Beginning: C_mm_nc_ng
2. The length of time to give forewarning: T_rm _f n_t_c_

3. A new clause added to a contract on a separate piece of paper: R_d_r
4. A written declaration made under oath: _ff_d_v_t
5. Documentary proof of giving up a right: W_ _v_r
6. To fail to do something agreed on in the contract: Br_ _ch _f c_ntr_ct
7. The date all the work specified in the contract is completed: C_mpl_t_ _n d_t_
8. To end a contract: T_rm_n_t_

## D. COMPOUND NOUNS (Just for a little change)

↘ *1 out of the 3 proposals is incorrect. Which one is wrong?*

1. Human / natural / minerals: RESOURCES
2. Travelling / gift / lunch: VOUCHER
3. Staff / apple / money: TURNOVER
4. Consumer / self / myself: CONFIDENCE
5. Wine / coffee / sherry: GLASS
6. Peanut / traffic / strawberry: JAM
7. Cell phone's / item / room: NUMBER
8. Greeting / phone / credit: CARD
9. Box / post / tickets: OFFICE
10. Parenting / quality / self: CONTROL
11. Exchange / interests / unemployment: RATE
12. Market / ware / fair: SHARE
13. Dining / sitting / bathing: ROOM
14. Red / pink / dry: WINE
15. A three-hour / five-minutes / half-hour: MEETING

# 4 Meetings & Appointments

## A. LET ME LOOK IN MY DIARY

↘ *Put the date in the boxes and decide which day Bill and Katie are going to be able to meet.*

| | | | | | | |
|---|---|---|---|---|---|---|
| Monday | 30 | 6 | 13 | 20 | 27 | 4 |
| Tuesday | 31 | 7 | 14 | 21 | 28 | 5 |
| Wednesday | 1 JUNE | 8 | 15 | 22 | 29 | 6 ABOVE PAR |
| Thursday | 2 | 9 | 16 | 23 | 30 | 7 |
| Friday | 3 TODAY | 10 | 17 | 24 | 1 JULY | 8 |
| Saturday | 4 | 11 | 18 | 25 | 2 | 9 |
| Sunday | 5 | 12 | 19 | 26 | 3 | 10 |

**B:** So Katie, are you coming to the "Above Par" conference in St. Andrews?
**K:** Is that about golf, or how to be better than everyone else?!
**B:** The latter of course! By the way, I had a great round of golf the day before yesterday!! **1.** ______
**K:** I played 3 days ago – and I won!! **2.** ______ So, when is this conference?
**B:** On the flier it says 06/07/10.
**K:** Yes, but be careful, in Europe that means 6th July, 2010, whereas in the USA it means June 7th, so which date are you talking about?!
**B:** July, I'm sure it's in July.
**K:** Maybe we should meet up before to discuss what questions we want to ask.
**B:** That's a good idea – let me look in my diary... I'm pretty booked up, I'm afraid. →

→ OK, so today's the 3rd.
Tomorrow and the day after tomorrow – well, that's this weekend! **3.** ______
On Monday I'm off to Rome. **4.** ______ Next weekend I'm going to brain training. **5.** ______
The weekend after that it's my wife's birthday. **6.** ______ I do try and keep my weekends free.
Next week from Wednesday to Friday I'll be in NYC. **7.** ______
I have sales meetings every other Tuesday from 31st May onwards. **8.** ______
We're off on a week's holiday in a fortnight's time. **9.** ______
In 3 day's time I'll be at a trade fair in London for a couple of days. **10.** ______
I have meetings with suppliers every last Thursday and Friday of the month. **11.** ______
**K:** Wow! You are busy! Have a great holiday. I won't be free right in the middle of the month – we have a quality audit day and night for 3 days as from 15th. **12.** ______ I'm dreading it!!

**B:** I reckon we need a couple of days to get sorted out and for travelling over to Scotland, so the Monday and Tuesday before is out, I'm afraid. **13.** ______

**K:** Well, that's easy - we only have one date possible!! **14.** ______ I'm looking forward to catching up on everything.

## B. SUNRISE or SUNSET, DAWN or DUSK?

↘ *Match up the words / expressions in the two columns.*

| | |
|---|---|
| **1.** A decade • | • **A.** Half an hour |
| **2.** 2 weeks • | • **B.** A month |
| **3.** 12am • | • **C.** A year |
| **4.** 7.40 • | • **D.** Nineteen ninety-five |
| **5.** 60 minutes • | • **E.** 10 years |
| **6.** 28/29/30/31 days • | • **F.** Half past two |
| **7.** 2012 • | • **G.** Seven minutes past three |
| **8.** 12pm • | • **H.** A quarter of an hour |
| **9.** 06:00 • | • **I.** Midnight |
| **10.** 7 days • | • **J.** Quarter past four |
| **11.** 15:07 • | • **K.** Midday |
| **12.** 30 minutes • | • **L.** Twenty-Twelve |
| **13.** 16:15 • | • **M.** A minute |
| **14.** 1995 • | • **N.** A week |
| **15.** 24 hours • | • **O.** An hour |
| **16.** 10:35 • | • **P.** A fortnight |
| **17.** 12 months • | • **Q.** A day |
| **18.** 15 minutes • | • **R.** Six o'clock |
| **19.** 60 seconds • | • **S.** Twenty-five to eleven |
| **20.** 14:30 • | • **T.** Twenty to eight |

## C. THE MEETING HAS BEEN DEFERRED

***Match the right word / expression to the dates.***

• cancel • arrange • defer • bring / put forward • postpone • be off • give a week's warning • set up • fix • put back

Organise the meeting for 18th March, 2009 ..........................................................................
Watch out! Meeting in 7 days, time! ..........................................................................
12th June, 2010, to 6th July, 2010 ..........................................................................
9th November, 2009, to 29th October, 2010 ..........................................................................
8th January, 2009, to never! ..........................................................................

## D. KINDS OF MEETING

***Sort out the letters to find the word.***

**1.** A meeting every 3 months: AEQYTRURL = ..........................................................................
**2.** Key executives who arrange the order of business: ENSIGERT TCTEMIMEO = ..................................
**3.** Annual gathering of directors and stockholders: GAM = ..........................................................
**4.** Like a management committee: ORADB = ..........................................................................
**5.** A short meeting before and after an event: FREGNIIB / EIDGNIFERB = ........................................
**6.** A group of people who meet regularly to discuss a certain subject: DSUYT RUOPG = ...................
**7.** A group of people who conduct research in certain areas: HKITN NAKT = ......................................
**8.** A small team with responsibility for a specific subject: TSKA RFCOE = ......................................
**9.** A small group designated to discuss a specific matter: MTOETMEIC = ..........................................
**10.** A meeting to exchange ideas: ASNEIRM = ..........................................................................

## E. ORGANISATION

***Running the meeting – put in vowels to complete the words.***

**1.** Can you make sure everyone is ..v....l..bl.. on 20th August?
**2.** We have to find a s....t...bl.. venue. How about the boardroom?
**3.** After that, we must n..t..fy all the participants.
**4.** Someone must prepare the ..g..nd.. so we know what we'll be discussing.
**5.** Mr. Jones, do you think you could take the ch....r?
**6.** We don't have all day, I think we should set a time l..m..t.
**7.** Could someone take down the m..n..t..s?
**8.** We'll have a show of hands, and some have voted by pr..xy vote.
**9.** At the end, leave time for AOB, in other words "..ny ..th..r b..s..n..ss".
**10.** So, to conclude, I would like to s..m ..p what we have decided.
**11.** We must keep a r..c..rd (of the meeting).
**12.** Could we please have the r..p..rt by Friday?
**13.** I hope everyone understands what t..sk they are responsible for!
**14.** We'll have a c..nf..r..nc.. c..ll next week to save travelling expenses.

# Communicating

## F. A FEW USEFUL EXPRESSIONS or TIME IS MONEY

*Match the thought balloon to the expression.*

**a.** This could be the way we can progress.

**b.** I'll let you know my answer in a few days.

**c.** We're not getting anywhere. Let's go to the next point.

**d.** That is just not possible!

**e.** We just don't understand each other!

**f.** Time to end this meeting!

**g.** If I could just interrupt for a minute...

**h.** I think I know why you are saying what you are saying!

**i.** If we examine what the situation is...

**j.** Let's vote on this.

**k.** Can we run through all of that?

**l.** Time to bring things to a close.

**m.** Shall we come back to this at a later date?

**n.** We are getting away from the main subject.

**1.** We are not on the same wavelength.
**2.** I can see where you're coming from.
**3.** Let's take a rain check.
**4.** Let's have a show of hands.
**5.** I'll get back to you on that one.
**6.** Let's wrap up here.
**7.** Can we recap?
**8.** If we were to take stock of the situation...
**9.** Let's call it a day.
**10.** That's just not on!
**11.** I think we're drifting off the point.
**12.** Could I come in here, please?
**13.** Let's move on, shall we?
**14.** This could be a way forward.

# 5 Negotiating

## A. A BIT OF BARGAINING

↘ *Try and put the 21 sentences into the right box. Don't forget to put the verb in the right tense!*

**1.** It's such a good bargain.
**2.** Would you be willing to...?
**3.** We've hit a sticking point.
**4.** We have an excellent reputation.
**5.** As a rule we don't....
**6.** Let's make a counter-offer.
**7.** The main problem here is...
**8.** We've reached a stalemate.
**9.** Our products are built to last.
**10.** We're so pleased to be doing business with you.
**11.** What would you say if...?
**12.** We'll have to talk them into it.
**13.** Unless you can... we cannot...
**14.** They have withdrawn their offer.
**15.** I really think you should look the agreement over again.
**16.** Could you...? In return we could...
**17.** Shall we clarify?
**18.** We are devoted to quality.
**19.** We could only accept this if you...
**20.** Let me spell out our conditions.
**21.** We must win them over.

| |
|---|
| **A: Seeing what the other party really thinks** |
| **B: Explaining the limits** |
| **C: Making conditions** |
| **D: Bargaining points** |
| **E: Persuading** |
| **F: Driving the message home** |
| **G: Nothing left to do** |

## B. 6 MORE CONFUSING WORDS

↘ *Choose between the two words to complete a) and b). You may need to conjugate the verb.*

**1. Sensible / sensitive: a)** She's so .............................. – she never gets stressed.
**b)** He's really .............................., we all talk our problems through with him.
**2. Shadow / shade: a)** It's really hot, shall we put the table in the ..............................?
**b)** When I was a child, we played at jumping our ..............................
**3. Speak / talk: a)** Please don't .............................. during the presentation.
**b)** She .............................. good French.
**4. Teach / learn: a)** Could you .............................. that secretary how to type?!
**b)** Will you never .............................. not to slam the door?
**5. Wander / wonder: a)** Please don't .............................. on the way home – I worry.
**b)** People often .............................. how he puts up with his boss.
**6. Watch / look at: a)** .............................. that awful building over there!!
**b)** The average man .............................. more TV than the average woman.

## C. I JUST HAD A THOUGHT....!

*Match the sentence in the "thought" balloon to what you might actually say.*

**1.** We need an estimate.
**2.** If you ... we may...
**3.** Our aim is...
**4.** I'm not quite sure – I need to think more about it.
**5.** We can't do more than that.
**6.** The company will never let us do that.
**7.** Our position is this...
**8.** We must have a delivery deadline.
**9.** No way!
**10.** We are really worried about...

**A.** Let me outline our position...
**B.** We are hoping to achieve...
**C.** Our main worry is this...
**D.** Could you quote me for 6 tons of...
**E.** Can you guarantee delivery for...
**F.** On condition that you make regular orders, we could offer you a discount.
**G.** We could not go beyond that.
**H.** I'm afraid that's out of the question.
**I.** I'm afraid that's not company policy.
**J.** We would have to get back to you on that one.

# 6 Presentations & Graphs

## A. EQUIPMENT FOR A PRESENTATION

*Find the word in the snake.*

dataprojectorwhiteboardflipchartscreenpointeroverhead
projectorslideshandout

**1.** Something to give out to the attendees.
**2.** To project onto or display your presentation.
**3.** Transparencies.
**4.** "Paper board".
**5.** A stick to point things out.
**6.** What your teacher used in school, but white.
**7.** A computer-linked system for displaying.
**8.** An older system for displaying.

## B. WHAT KIND OF GRAPH or CHART SHALL I USE?

*Match the word to the picture.*

- Flowchart
- Pie chart
- Run chart / line graph
- Value stream mapping
- Spreadsheet
- Organisation chart
- Bar chart
- Diagram

1
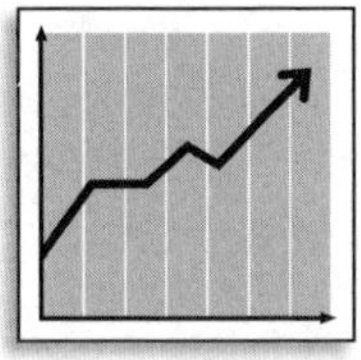

2
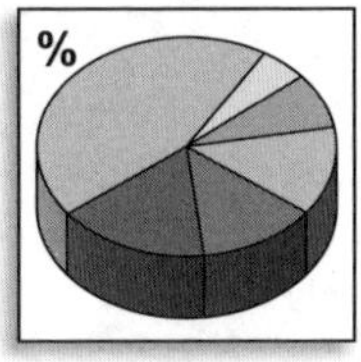


3
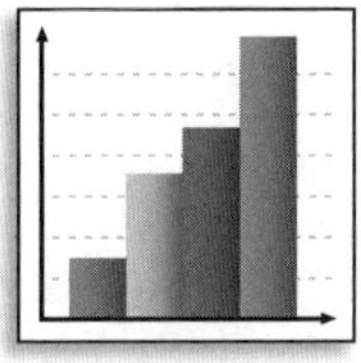

4

5
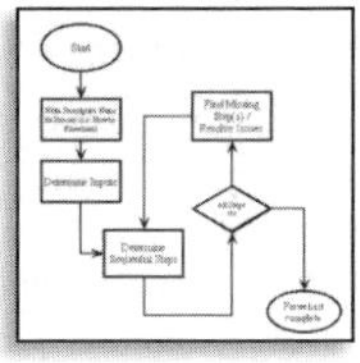

6
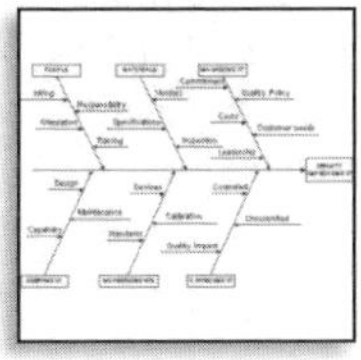

7
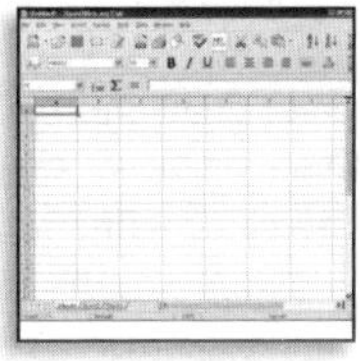

8
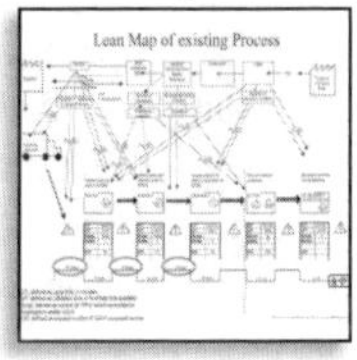

## C. UPS AND DOWNS

*Put the following expressions into the right column.*

**1.** Climb steadily
**2.** Sharp fall
**3.** Stand at
**4.** Bottom out
**5.** Slump considerably
**6.** Peak at
**7.** Pick up slightly
**8.** Level out
**9.** Flatten out gradually
**10.** Substantial plunge
**11.** Drop noticeably
**12.** Steep rise

| Go up / improve | Go down / deteriorate | Even out / remain stable | Top and bottom |
|---|---|---|---|
| | | | |

# 7 Small Talk

## A. A LITTLE SOCIAL CHIT-CHAT

*Choose the right answer(s).*

**1.** Have a good trip / journey / travel.
**2.** How do you do? I'm pleased / glad / happy to meet you.
**3.** Shall we / will we / let's break for lunch. That's a good idea.
**4.** Would you like / do you like / like you a cup of coffee?
**5.** How are you? It's nice to meet / see / welcome you again. →

→ **6.** I'm afraid / I'm sorry but / excuse me he will be late.
**7.** I have an appointment / a date / a meeting with Mr. Smith.
**8.** See you later / earlier / on Friday.
**9.** How's the company / your hotel like / business?
**10.** Welcome to BirminghamMister / Mr. / Mrs. / Miss / Ms. Smith / Peter.
**11.** I am not agree / do not agree / I am not ok = I think it's a bad idea.
**12.** What's your line of business? / What do you? / What business are you in?
**13.** What's your full name? Joan Smith / Joan / Ms. Smith.
**14.** Could we fix / arrange / take an appointment?
**15.** I do / am appreciate you coming so early.
**16.** How about an appointment on the 26$^{th}$? Does that suit you? / Does that convenience you? / Is that convenient?

## B. WHAT'S THE TEMPERATURE? (In degrees Celsius or Fahrenheit!)

↘ ***Put these words in the right order from the coldest to the hottest.***

warm – chilly – hot – below freezing – mild – boiling hot – freezing cold – cool

........................................................................................................................

## C. WHAT WONDERFUL WEATHER!

↘ ***Match the comment to the weather condition.***

**1.** Oh, I must look at the weather forecast. •
**2.** It's going to be a scorcher today. •
**3.** They say there'll be showers later. •
**4.** It's been raining really heavily. •
**5.** Are you afraid of thunderstorms? •
**6.** Do you realize it's minus 15?! •
**7.** It's cold – it's the wind, I think. •
**8.** It's overcast again this morning. •
**9.** Look, raindrops and sunshine together. •
**10.** There's been a lot of snow recently. •
**11.** I can't see a thing ahead of me! •
**12.** Too much water and we get a flood. •
**13.** The blizzard brought a lot of snow. •
**14.** I prefer a nice, clear cold spell with frost. •
**15.** It's hot, a gentle breeze would be nice. •
**16.** The flowers are drooping in the heat wave. •

• **A.** Is it foggy or is it smog from the industrial estate?
• **B.** The road conditions will be bad – it'll be icy.
• **C.** I'd rather wait and see what the day brings.
• **D.** So do I, I hate slush after a snowstorm.
• **E.** After the damage from the hail in the spring.
• **F.** I'm fed up with this cloudy weather!
• **G.** We'll take an umbrella – it's only drizzling for now
• **H.** Yes, but don't wish too hard - you'll get a hurricane!
• **I.** Be careful about an avalanche if you go skiing.
• **J.** We'll need the air conditioner.
• **K.** But not enough and we get a drought!
• **L.** No, I love the lightning and the thunder.
• **M.** Yes, let's find the end of the rainbow.
• **N.** Yes, the wind chill factor is high today.
• **O.** Good, there'll be lots of puddles to jump in!
• **P.** Now the snow's turned into sleet, so it'll melt.

## D. COLOURFUL EXPRESSIONS

*Put the idiom or expression into the right colour box.*

| Black | Black & blue | Black & white | Brown | Blue | Grey |
|---|---|---|---|---|---|
| | | | | | |

| Green | Pink | Red | White | Yellow | Rainbow |
|---|---|---|---|---|---|
| | | | | | |

**1.** He's been put on the blacklist – nobody wants to employ him now.
**2.** They have earmarked that meadow for the new factory - it's a Greenfield site.
**3.** I saw red when the boss told me I had to do the spreadsheet all over again!
**4.** We were surprised, the inspector arrived right out of the blue!
**5.** He's full of bruises, black and blue, after the rugby match.
**6.** She's always chasing rainbows, but I bet she'll get there in the end.
**7.** He's been given a pink slip – the poor chap has lost his job.
**8.** There used to be an industrial site here before; it was contaminated so now it's a brownfield site.
**9.** Could you put that down in black and white so it's clear?
**10.** No building is allowed in that green belt.
**11.** It's a bit of a grey area – nobody really knows the answer.
**12.** There's an awful lot of red tape involved in setting up a company.
**13.** That is a really sensationalist newspaper – part of the yellow press.
**14.** He'll get grey hair with all that stress.
**15.** I argued about it until I was blue in the face!
**16.** He talks a blue streak, I don't understand what he says at all.
**17.** She was tickled pink when she got her promotion.
**18.** They rolled out the red carpet for new company president.
**19.** He told a white lie to avoid hurting her feelings.
**20.** I'm really in their black books since I forgot to go to the opening ceremony.

## 1 Travelling

### A. GLOBE-TROTTING

↘ *Match the word to the definition.*

1. Travel •
2. Journey •
3. Trip •
4. Tour •
5. Voyage •

- **A.** A short way there and back, e.g. business ..., a .... to the bank
- **B.** Going from A to B by car, bus, etc. (a verb)
- **C.** A long way to a distant place, which is often glamorous
- **D.** Long distance, potentially for a discovery, could be tiring or not much fun
- **E.** Go around and visit

### B. A TOUCH OF ECOTOURISM

↘ *Look at the advert and replace the underlined words by one of the words below.*

- Traveller's checks
- Peak-season
- All-inclusive
- Vacancies
- Vacation
- Departure date
- Accommodation
- Valid passport
- Transfers
- Affordable
- Off-season
- Package deals

**DISCOVER LOCAL CULTURES, GO ON A WILDERNESS ADVENTURE...**

Without boasting we offer the best **1.** tour where everything is arranged by us on the market.

Thinking about taking a **2.** a period of time for leisure and pleasure abroad?

We have a huge selection of **3.** low cost and unforgettable breaks.

Just look through our catalogue for details about our **4.** where everything is included trips and tours. Choose your dates, **5.** the season where rates are lowest or **6.** the season where rates are highest, and your destination - then call us to discuss **7.** where you will stay, we will check for **8.** empty rooms, flights and **9.** the journey from the airport to your hotel(s), and leisure or tourism (flora, fauna and cultural heritage) occupations during your stay.

We look after everything, from visas and **10.** travel identification which is not out of date, to drinks at the bar when you arrive.

Worried about carrying foreign currency around? We will get you cash at the best exchange rate, and organise your **11.** a check representing money in the local currency for you.

Just tell us your **12.** the day you want to leave – and we will reserve everything for you (and you only have to pay a 10% deposit) – nothing could be more like a real holiday!

## C. FLYING OUT

↘ ***Follow the flowchart – and put in all the options.***

1 | 2 | Book a ticket | 3 | 4

5 | 6 | 7 | 8

9 | Check the baggage allowance – Size and weight of | 10

If overweight, pay excess baggage

11 | 12 | Buy a ticket & pay the airfare | 13 | 14

Go to the airport. Go to the right terminal.
Go past "Passport holders only beyond this point".
With

15 | 16 | 17 | 18

Listen for announcement "Passengers for Flight AB312 to Canton, please go to Gate Number 15". Gate Number 15 for 13.20 flight to Canton.
With

19 | 20 | 21 | 22 | 23 | 24

If you have travelled to a difference time zone, just hope that ...

25 | 26

**A.** E-ticket
**B.** Direct flight
**C.** Briefcase / suitcase
**D.** The plane goes to the runway
**E.** Passport and visa
**F.** Customs
**G.** You don't have jetlag
**H.** Take off
**I.** Hold luggage
**J.** Check-in at airport
**K.** Round trip
**L.** Go to the departure lounge
**M.** Hand luggage
**N.** Show boarding card
**O.** Land at destination
**P.** One way
**Q.** The time difference isn't too much
**R.** Travel agent
**S.** There is a stopover
**T.** Domestic flight
**U.** On-line check-in
**V.** Long haul flight (Long distance)
**W.** Board the plane
**X.** Short haul flight (Short distance)
**Y.** International flight
**Z.** Immigration

## D. PROBLEMS AND YET MORE PROBLEMS

↘ ***Choose the right word to put in the dialogue.***

A: So, did you have a good flight, Bill?

B: Well, I've know better. Can you imagine, I think I had every hassle possible – it took me 48 hours to get to Sydney!!

A: Instead of the usual 24!! You poor thing – aeroplanes aren't very spacious at the best of times – there's no leg room at all. So, what happened?

B: Well, I got to the airport on time as usual. I went to check-in and was told I was **1.** overheavy / overweight!

A: How rude!

B: Well no, I don't mean me - my baggage was overweight so I had to pay excess baggage fees.

A: Well, was your flight on time, or was it **2.** delayed / in late?

B: Worse than that, it was **3.** annulled / cancelled – there was too much fog! So I had to get on the next flight to Dubai (where I was stopping over anyway for a couple of hours).

A: There are cancellations for any reason! Well, did you manage to get your connection to Sydney?

B: What do you think? When I arrived, I was told by the flight attendant that the first flight out was **4.** surbooked / overbooked, so I had to wait for the next one – which was the next day!

A: So, you stopped overnight in Dubai – that's nice!

B: Well, not really, it took me hours to get out of the airport because of special **5.** customs regulations / custom regulations. It was my fault, I'd left my baggage unattended.

A: Yes, and you were carrying all those toiletries to show customers, too – that can't have been easy.

B: But that wasn't the end of my troubles. When I got to the airport the next day, I was told my ticket was **6.** invalid / invalidated, and I had to buy another one! And if that wasn't enough, when we got on the plane at last, there was suddenly a message from the **7.** air host / steward saying "The pilot would like to apologise to passengers, but we have been **8.** rerouted / reroaded to Perth".

A: Sounds like a gruelling journey - and all that for a 2-hour meeting! It can't have been worth it – I'd try a conference call next time!

## E. ON THE ROAD AGAIN

↘ ***Put the conversation in the right order. There is a different print for each of the 2 speakers.***

**1.** Excuse me, I'm lost. How do I get to the Highway Hotel?
**2.** The length of stay depends on you - there's both long-term and short-term parking.
**3.** How long will it take?
**4.** You might do better to go to the car park for now – there are lots of parking spaces.
**5.** Do you think you could draw me a map?
**6.** Why not, I'm a hitchhiker at heart. Let me just get my backpack!
**7.** So we might get stuck in a traffic jam?

**8.** I'm afraid you've gone the wrong way – you'll have to turn round – mind the guardrail!!
**9.** Well, it'll take you ten minutes because of the one-way system.
**10.** Well, it's 5 o'clock, so it's rush hour.
**11.** Well, as I said, there's a one-way system, an overpass, pedestrian precincts and the like.
**12.** Here you are.... Thank you so much. Can we give you a lift anywhere?
**13.** How far is it?
**14.** Yes, you might. Whatever you do, don't go in the bus lane – the police are very strict on that.
**15.** Is it a long-term car park? We could maybe leave the car there and take the tram to the hotel.
**16.** It's about 7 miles from here.
**17.** Of course I can. Have you got a pen and paper?
**18.** Thanks for warning us!!
**19.** Is it easy to find?
**20.** Is it a long way from here?

..........................................................................................................................

## CAR HIRE / RENTAL

↘ ***First, find out what kinds of car you can rent in the word snake?***

Minieconomycompactintermediatestandardfullsizepremiumluxuryconvertible sportscarlimousineminivanfullsizevanpickuptrucksportutilityvehicle stationwagon

..........................................................................................................................

..........................................................................................................................

↘ ***Now, look at the needs listed A-J below the box, and tick where appropriate.***

| | | | |
|---|---|---|---|
| **1.** Unlimited mileage | D | **6.** Keys available at airport | |
| **2.** Comprehensive insurance | | **7.** 20% deposit before taking the car | |
| **3.** Full tank | | **8.** Drop-off charge | |
| **4.** Automatic transmission | | **9.** Low rates | |
| **5.** Manual gear box | | **10.** Clean drivers licence | |

If we can satisfy your request, we shall ask you to fill in a more detailed form.

**A.** I can bring the car back to where I pick it up from.
**B.** I like to feel in touch and in control of the car when I change gears.
**C.** The company is paying, so I don't have to worry about how much it costs.
**D.** I want to travel as far as I like, with no limits.
**E.** I shall be arriving by train.
**F.** I want to be fully covered in case of an accident.
**G.** I have no points taken off my driving licence.
**H.** I'll be using my company credit card to pay, so won't need to make a down payment.
**I.** I don't want an easy-to-use car with only two pedals.
**J.** There's a petrol station just near the rental agency, so I can fill up quickly.

## G. TAKING A TAXI (or CAB)

↘ *Are the following sentences true or false?*

**1.** If you say to a taxi driver, "Keep the change", you want some money back. ...............
**2.** To ask for your destination, the taxi driver will often say, "Where to, sir?" ...............
**3.** The driver has the right to refuse or accept the hire. ...............
**4.** A taxi will never give you a receipt. ...............
**5.** Many taxis in Paris won't accept payment by credit card. ...............
**6.** In Toronto, taxis are prohibited from taking luggage in the cabin of the vehicle. ...............
**7.** In Singapore, there may be an extra charge at peak periods, midnight and public holidays. ...............
**8.** The taxi fare from Rome to the airport, for 2 people, is about €500. ...............
**9.** In New York you can whistle for a cab from the sidewalk. ...............
**10.** You should never wave a cab down in Europe. ...............
**11.** You should never go to a taxi stand to get a licensed taxi. ...............
**12.** There is a set rate for the taxi fare from many airports to the nearest town centre. ...............
**13.** In some countries, you can negotiate the taxi fare. ...............
**14.** You should never leave a tip under 20%. ...............

## H. SO THE TRAIN TAKES THE STRAIN

↘ *Can you find the answer to the question?*

**1.** How much is a first class to London, please?
**2.** What's the difference between a first class and a second class to Swindon, please?
**3.** When does the first train leave in the morning?
**4.** Where did you say I should get my season ticket?
**5.** Why are there so many cars in that car park?
**6.** Whose bicycle is that?
**7.** Who wants to have the window seat?
**8.** Which platform does the train for Fairfield leave from?
**9.** What time is the 8:45 for Petersfield expected?
**10.** So, where are you sitting?
**11.** What's the best way to get to the airport?
**12.** What did the rail staff get angry about?
**13.** How do you know that woman?
**14.** Do you think you could give me a hand?
**15.** Shall we meet in the waiting room?

**16.** Oh no – did you hear that announcement?
**17.** What will you do if you don't take the train for the return journey?
**18.** Don't you think you'd better get off the train now?
**19.** Did you manage to change your ticket?
**20.** How are you going to get there in time for a breakfast meeting?

**A.** We get on the subway at the same time every morning and evening.
**B.** I prefer to sit in the aisle, there's more leg room.
**C.** It's ok – the guard hasn't blown his whistle yet.
**D.** Single or return?
**E.** Take the shuttle – it goes every quarter of an hour.
**F.** It's ok – I've got a fully refundable ticket.
**G.** The commuter train leaves from here.
**H.** I'm going to take a sleeper on the overnight train.
**I.** I'm in carriage number 4, seat number 28.
**J.** There's a milk train at 5:05.
**K.** It's running late – about 9:20, I think.
**L.** Unfortunately not – look at the small print, it says "Ticket exchange subject to limited availability".
**M.** About £20.00.
**N.** Oh yes, the train is going to be delayed.
**O.** I think it's platform 3.
**P.** Yes of course, it is rather heavy to get up on the luggage rack.
**Q.** It's mine – sorry, I'll put it on the cycle rack.
**R.** There's a contact point in the centre of the station – that would be better.
**S.** For the commuter train, just pick it up at the ticket office.
**T.** I was leaning out of the window – it's forbidden.

## I. ON THE BUS

↘ ***Sort out the mixed-up letters to complete the sentence.***

**1.** The price of commuting by bus is awful – Passenger ASFER ................ go up every month!
**2.** There were too many people on the bus this morning – it was really WERDODC ................
**3.** In England, people stand in line (queue) at the USB OSPT ................
**4.** It doesn't stop at every village, this is a HUHTGOR ................ bus.
**5.** We're lucky, there's a very good Bus ECVREIS ................ to the town centre.
**6.** We travelled round London on the top floor of the OBUELD CREEKD ................
**7.** To save time, I don't buy a ticket every day – I have a ENAOSS IETTKC ................ instead.
**8.** I'm sorry I'm late this morning – although I ran fast, I ISDMES ................ the bus.

## J. WE TOOK THE FERRY

*The rain has damaged the postcard – can you fill in the gaps?*

| | |
|---|---|
| *Amazing trip – we took the High Speed f.................. from the end of the pier over to the little harbor on the Island. On the way we were overtaken by the h.................. (but that only takes f.................. p.................. and we had our car). Really funny – we bumped into John and Ros in the b.................. l.................. so we travelled over with them – it was only a 30-minute c.................. but we had time for a quick drink. It was a lovely s.................. and the sea was c.................. (Pete hates it when it's r.................. and there are big waves!)* | *Pete and Joan Smith*<br>*22 Wilson Street*<br>*Linton*<br>*Kent* |

**a)** Ship **b)** Ferry **c)** Hovercraft **d)** Rough **e)** Foot passengers **f)** Crossing **g)** Boarding lounge **h)** Calm

## K. HOMONYMS FOR HOPPING AROUND

*Or "travel homonyms"*
*Choose between the two words to complete a) and b).*

**1. Aisle / isle: a)** Would you like an ............... or a window seat?
**b)** The ............... of Wight is wonderful for sailing.
**2. Allowed / aloud: a)** He read the itinerary ...............
**b)** Is smoking .............. in here?
**3. Find / fined: a)** He didn't ............... the speeding ticket.
**b)** He was ............... for speeding.
**4. For / four: a)** I'm waiting ............... the bus.
**b)** I've been here ............... hours.
**5. Sail / sale: a)** There's a very big ............... on that boat.
**b)** There's the spring ............... at the stores.
**6. Threw / through: a)** We drove ............... the housing estate.
**b)** He ............... the rubbish overboard – that's awful!

## L. BOOKING HOTEL ACCOMMODATION

*Choose the right word(s) in the letter.*

**BLAKENY & Co.**
**24 West Street, LONDON**
* * * * *

Plush People's Hotel
Luxury Street
Cape Town

24th October, 20..

Dear Sir / Madam

I am writing to make a reservation for 6 double bedrooms with bath from Monday 15th November to Friday 19th November **1)** included / inclusive / comprehensive (4 nights), in the name of Mr. James Blakeny. We require **2)** half-board / half pension with English breakfast.
Could you please confirm your **3)** tarif / rates (I think we are in a peak-rate period), and answer the following questions?
What time do we have to **4)** check in / inregister / sign in?
What time do we have to **5)** check out / outregister / sign out?
Which hotel **6)** facilities / equipment are available to guests at this time of the year?
Do you have special rates for groups (we shall be 12 altogether)?
Are all taxes included in the price?

Please find enclosed a check as agreed for the deposit. Could you please confirm this booking by return of post? I look forward to hearing from you.

Yours faithfully,

## M. CHOOSE YOUR HOTEL ROOM

*Match the room to the definition.*

| | |
|---|---|
| Double • | • With a bedroom and a sitting room |
| En-suite • | • With two single beds |
| Single • | • With one bed for two people |
| Suite • | • For parents and children (sometimes two adjoining rooms) |
| Twin • | • Just for one person (one single bed) |
| Family • | • With private bathroom (with bath or shower) |

## N. WHAT KIND OF ACCOMMODATION?

*Match one (or more) of the words below to the description.*

**1.** In the capital
**2.** In the outskirts of the city
**3.** In a nearby suburb
**4.** In the countryside
**5.** Full-board
**6.** Half-board
**7.** All-inclusive
**8.** B&B
**9.** Self-catering
**10.** Motel
**11.** Luxury hotel
**12.** Budget hotel
**13.** Youth hostel
**14.** Holiday cottage
**15.** Apartment hotel
**16.** Condo hotel

**A.** Backpacking around Europe and need somewhere reasonable to stay? Try our hospitality in a single or shared room.
**B.** A sea view and open fireplace just add to the charm of this little seaside house to rent.
**C.** Right in the centre of one of Europe's chief historical towns, we offer the most comfortable and sumptuous hotel you are ever likely to stay in. Everything is included, from delicious dinners to full use of the wellness centre.
**D.** Park your car just next to your bedroom and sleep without worries. In a small town within easy commuting distance of the city centre.
**E.** Come to our house, and during breakfast listen to the birds sing on a sunny spring morning in the unspoiled countryside. If you are looking for peace and quiet in a secluded spot...
**F.** No need to worry about cooking on this holiday – every meal is catered for.
**G.** Just away from the city centre, this hotel is good value for money – cheaper than all the competition.
**H.** You don't want to be stuck in a tiny hotel room? We offer 1 or 2 bedrooms with sitting room and kitchenette. If you like, you can even have breakfast and one other meal in the dining room on the ground floor.
**I.** Try something new. In this hotel you will find both owners and guests – half the apartments are privately owned, and the other half are for renting out.
**J.** Find ski resorts too expensive? It's of course much cheaper to do your own catering and to rent a furnished flat, 5 minutes from the centre in a beautiful valley village.

## O. CUSTOMARY COMPLAINTS

*Match the beginning to the end of the sentence.*

1. The "Do not disturb" sign was ignored and •
2. The chambermaid didn't •
3. The facilities were not the same •
4. The heated swimming pool •
5. The machines in the fitness room •
6. Broadband didn't work •
7. The receptionist yesterday •
8. I kept calling room service •
9. We asked for a wake-up call •
10. We were charged a supplement for the mini-bar. •
11. There's a dreadful smell, •
12. This bill is high! I'm afraid I think •
13. The bellhop took •
14. I'm sorry but •
15. The carhop has •
16. We got stuck in the •

- **A.** someone has been smoking in our bedroom.
- **B.** were not working properly.
- **C.** my baggage to the wrong room.
- **D.** we were bothered by the maintenance man.
- **E.** elevator on the 15th floor.
- **F.** was extremely unfriendly.
- **G.** as those shown in the catalogue.
- **H.** but it never came through so we overslept.
- **I.** my key-card doesn't open my door.
- **J.** make up the beds properly.
- **K.** in the business centre.
- **L.** but we didn't have anything to drink.
- **M.** was freezing cold.
- **N.** but they didn't answer their phone.
- **O.** we were overcharged for our dinner last night.
- **P.** taken my Mercedes for a drive.

## P. LAUNDRY AND DRY CLEANING

↘ ***Put the clothes underneath into the right place on the list.***

**1.** vest (undershirt) **2.** jeans **3.** sweater / pullover **4.** bra **5.** shirt **6.** blouse **7.** raincoat **8.** skirt **9.** overcoat **10.** tie **11.** pants (underpants) **12.** t-shirt **13.** dress **14.** trousers **15.** socks **16.** sweatshirt **17.** tracksuit **18.** suit (jacket and trousers or jacket and skirt) **19.** pyjamas **20.** stockings **21.** tights **22.** nightdress **23.** hat **24.** dressing gown **25.** cardigan **26.** shirt

| | | | | | | | |
|---|---|---|---|---|---|---|---|
| **GUEST LAUNDRY LIST** | | | | | | | |
| **NAME:** | | | | **ROOM N°:** | | **DATE:** | |
| Please do not pay cash | | | Laundry collected before 6am will be returned the same day | | | | |
| Please send this list with your laundry and mark the service required | | | | | | | |
| Finished garments required: On hanger ❑ Folded ❑ | | | | | | Laundry<br>Dry cleaning | ❑<br>❑ |
| Guest Count | Hotel Count | **GENTLEMEN** | Cleaning Charges | Guest Count | Hotel Count | **LADIES** | Cleaning Charges |
| | | **OUTDOOR** | | | | **OUTDOOR** | |
| | | **BUSINESS** | | | | **BUSINESS** | |
| | | **CASUAL** | | | | **CASUAL** | |
| | | **SPORTS** | | | | **SPORTS** | |
| | | **NIGHTWEAR** | | | | **NIGHTWEAR** | |
| | | **UNDERWEAR** | | | | **UNDERWEAR** | |
| PLEASE CLEAN MY SHOES ❑ | | | | | | | |
| The company shall not be responsible for items said to have been left with items. | | | | | | | |
| The company shall not be responsible for shrinkage, colour bleeding or damage due to inherent defects or worn out condition of fabric. In case of loss or damage by the company, compensation shall not exceed 10 times the cost of cleaning the articles. | | | | | | | |

## 2 Health Care

### A. KNOW YOUR BODY

↘ ***Match the following words to the right place on the body.***

**a)** chest
**b)** hand
**c)** leg
**d)** knee
**e)** head
**f)** elbow
**g)** thumb
**h)** back
**i)** toe
**j)** stomach
**k)** eye
**l)** heel
**m)** shoulder
**n)** finger
**o)** tooth
**p)** neck
**q)** ear
**r)** foot
**s)** throat
**t)** ankle
**u)** hip
**v)** arm
**w)** wrist
**x)** nose
**y)** hair
**z)** eyebrow
**aa)** chin
**bb)** mouth

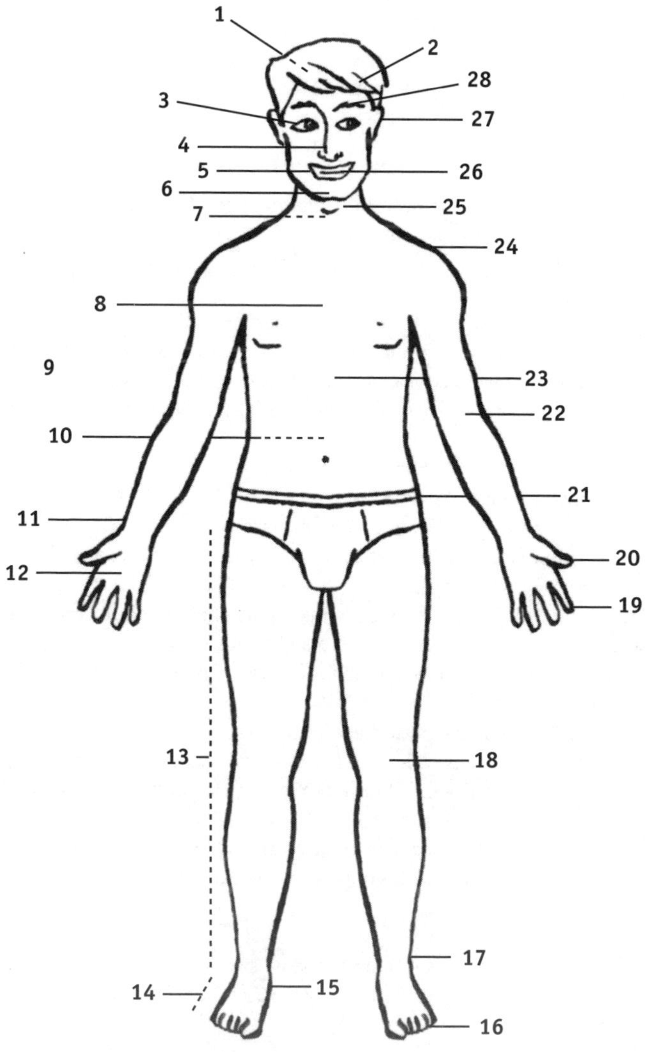

## B. SO, WHAT'S THE MATTER WITH YOU?

***Who is the patient, and who is he / she seeing – and where?***

Short / near-sighted person
G.P. (General practitioner)
Hospital
Doctor's surgery
Elderly person
Eye clinic
Psychologist's office
Patient waiting for surgery
Eye specialist
Senior citizen
Plastic surgeon
Housewife
Luxurious clinic
ENT specialist
Dentist's surgery
Star or model
In his successful practice
Psychologist
Anaesthetist
Student
Dentist
Man going deaf
Doctor

**1.** ........................... : Now that I'm over 70, I feel tired and breathless in the afternoon.
........................... : Well, I'm just going to take your blood pressure, could you pull up your sleeve? Well Mrs. Jones, I suggest you have a nap after lunch. You're in good health generally, no signs of any cardio-vascular disease.

**2.** ........................... : I went out for a drink with all the other undergraduates last night.
........................... : I know you don't have any drug dependence, so my diagnosis is that you are suffering from an over-enthusiastic intake of alcoholic substances – to simplify, you have a hangover.

**3.** ........................... : What with the children, the housekeeping, my job, the garden, the shopping and everything, this is just the last straw!
........................... : Now, you know that I am here to listen to everything you need to talk about. Mrs. Beehive, I think something must have upset you. Try taking a walk twice a day.

**4.** ........................... : Well, people have been taking my photograph for years, and I think I really need to have a facelift, a nose job, a few tucks here and there.
........................... : Let's have a look then – oh, have you got a healthy bank account?!

**5.** ........................... : I've got the most dreadful toothache.
........................... : Let me have a look.... Oh dear, this happens to older people. We'll need to do a lot of rebuilding in here I'm afraid. I'll have to reschedule your appointment.

**6.** ........................... : Will it take me long to go to sleep? I'm really terrified.
........................... : You won't even know what's happening. I put a mask on your face, you count to 10 and...

**7.** ........................... : I mishear everything everyone says – I must have problems with my ears.
........................... : You must be feeling very isolated but the solution is an easy one. I think you need a hearing aid, that's all.

8. ............................ : When I look at the TV it's all a blur!

............................ : I'm glad you came to the eye clinic. Let me just test your eyes ... I think you need a new pair of glasses.

## C. WHAT TREATMENT DO YOU NEED?

↘ ***Match the product to the description.***

1. A tablet •
2. A shot (USA) •
3. Ointment •
4. Herbal treatment •
5. Bug spray •
6. A sleeping pill •
7. Cream •
8. Cough syrup •
9. A plant brew •
10. A placebo •

- **A.** A small tablet to help you sleep
- **B.** A substance containing no active ingredients – a "sugar pill"
- **C.** A thick, sweet, sticky liquid to stop being chesty
- **D.** A dose of medicine given in a small pellet
- **E.** Plant products steeped in very hot water
- **F.** A remedy based on herbs
- **G.** An injection (UK)
- **H.** A soft solid for external use only
- **I.** A fine jet of liquid to avoid getting stung / bitten
- **J.** A semi-solid liquid for skin treatment

## D. HAVE YOU GOT MEDICAL INSURANCE?

↘ ***Make a word out of the mixed-up letters in the text.***

- Complementary
- Referrals
- Hearing
- Private
- Alternative
- Deductibles
- Premium
- Nursing
- Disability
- Prescription
- Welfare
- Screening

It is always wise to check out your medical insurance. Here are a few questions you should ask before taking out a 1) AERTVIP health insurance plan:

What does the State health system cover and is the 2) ERFEWAL system changing a lot at the moment?

Is 3) OECRAETYMNLPM health insurance very expensive? What is the annual 4) UEMRIMP?

Are the following included in a complementary health insurance plan?

- Osteopathy and other forms of 5) ETAEVIANRTL medicine
- 6) IIYBTDILAS or long-term nursing needs
- Health 7) CEGNIRNES and examinations
- Specialist treatments and 8) EREASRLRF
- Emergency care, hospitalisation and 9) SUNNIRG home care
- Physiotherapy and rehabilitative care
- 10) RCRITPNOSIEP costs
- Dental care, 11) EGRNHIA aids and vision care
- Mental health

Finally: What out of pocket or 12) DBECLSIUTED do I have to pay?

## 3 Wining & Dining

### A. EATING OUT

*Sort the following words into the right box.*

| | | | |
|---|---|---|---|
| Cheese | Waiting staff | Dessert | Chef |
| Business lunch | Highchair | A snack with mates | Pizza house |
| Booth | Wine waiter | Doggie bag | Steam |
| Boil | Drive-in | Cafeteria | Nibbles with drinks |
| Starter | Roast | Fry | Grill |
| Booster seat | Drinks at happy hour | Family dinner | Crockery |
| Glassware | Eatery | Smoke | Restaurant |
| Wine bar | Poach | Bartender | Waitress |
| Bake | Cutlery | Tablecloth | Tea room |
| Napkin | Waiter | Main course | |

| PLACES TO EAT | WHO YOU MIGHT SEE |
|---|---|
| | |

| VARIOUS KINDS OF MEAL | THE STAGES IN A MEAL |
|---|---|
| | |

| EQUIPMENT FOR MEALTIME | DIFFERENT WAYS OF COOKING |
| --- | --- |
| | |

## B. LET'S GO OUT FOR A MEAL

↘ ***Put each of the following little dialogues back into the right order.***

**A.**

**1.** I'd like to book a table for 4, please, for tomorrow evening.
**2.** Mr. Stir-Fry.
**3.** At 8 o'clock, please.
**4.** What time would you like your table?
**5.** Yes, in what name shall I make the reservation?

..........................................................................................................

**B.**

**1.** Good evening, could we have a table for 2, please.
**2.** I'll bring it so you can have a look.
**3.** Just water, please, we are all teetotallers.
**4.** So, what's on the menu today?
**5.** That's fine. So, still water or sparkling water?
**6.** Would you like some beverages?
**7.** Certainly, follow me.
**8.** I'm not! I'd love a glass of red wine.

.......................................................................................................... →

→ **C.**

**1.** Have you chosen your meal?
**2.** I'll take your dessert order now too, if I may.
**3.** Today's special is fried oysters with saffron cream. There are also lamb chops with mint.
**4.** Try the slimmer's salad.
**5.** Medium-rare please.
**6.** How is it cooked?
**7.** A savoury cheesy baked potato.
**8.** No meat for me thank you, I'm a vegetarian.
**9.** Not yet. What do you recommend?
**10.** Something very light for me please, I'm on a diet.
**11.** How would you like your meat cooked – rare, medium or well-done?
**12.** Very slowly, with fresh spring vegetables. It's a bit spicy.
**13.** I'll have a rump steak – what comes with it?
**14.** So the veggie risotto would be perfect for you.

**D.**

**1.** Excuse me, but the service is really a little slow, we ordered ages ago!
**2.** We've got a third problem! I'm afraid that the rice is a little burnt.
**3.** Would you like me to get you another one?
**4.** I'll bring you a fresh bread basket.
**5.** I'm sorry to complain again, but the wine is rather sweet – and it's corked!
**6.** I'll go and see the chef about that.
**7.** Last but not least - the bread is a bit stale!
**8.** Your starter is just coming now.
**9.** I'll get you another glass, Madam.
**10.** You won't believe this! I hate to say it, but the steak is a bit overcooked.

**E.**

**1.** Could you bring us the bill, please?
**2.** Yes, we take cash, checks and credit cards.
**3.** Is service included?
**4.** Excuse me, could you tell me where the rest rooms are, please?
**5.** Certainly – right away... How would you like to pay?
**6.** I'm afraid there seems to be a mistake - we have been overcharged for the water.
**7.** Well, a nice tip is always appreciated, sir.
**8.** Do you take credit cards?
**9.** Well sir, it is a very special kind of mineral water.

## C. WHAT'S IN THE REFRIGERATOR?

*Some things have been put on the wrong shelf! Put them back on the right shelf.*

**MEAT**
lamb – Brussels sprouts – pork – scallops – mussels – veal

**POULTRY**
egg – custard – goose – guinea fowl – green / red pepper – frogs' legs – duck

**VEGETABLES & SALAD**
cauliflower – beans – turnip – pheasant – leeks – asparagus – mushrooms – carrots – peas – lime potatoes – turkey – cabbage – spinach – tomato – lettuce – cucumber

**FISH & SEAFOOD**
trout – raspberry – shrimp – kipper – blackcurrant – prawns – pike – salmon

**GAME**
beef – hare – partridge – oysters – wild boar – venison – rabbit – mutton

**DESSERT / PUDDING & FRUIT**
avocado pear – pineapple – lemon – banana – chicken – pancake – apple – fruit salad – grapefruit – pear – grapes – lobster – ice cream – orange

## D. ARRANGING A WEDDING BANQUET

*Match the question to the answer.*

1. Is the groom planning a stag night?
2. Where's the reception being held?
3. How many people have been invited?
4. Are any celebrities going to attend?
5. What time do the festivities start?
6. Have you booked a caterer?
7. Have you chosen your outfit?
8. Should we have drinks in a tent in the garden?
9. What about the beverages?
10. Who's going to foot the bill for all this?!

- **A.** Just after the church of course.
- **B.** Not if the sun shines.
- **C.** Yes, and the bride's having a hen party, too.
- **D.** Tradition has it that the bride's family pick up the tab.
- **E.** At her house, of course.
- **F.** Yes, it's lovely – bright pink!
- **G.** At least 500.
- **H.** I chose a local chef who's famous for his culinary expertise.
- **I.** I've no idea – we've asked about twenty.
- **J.** Soft drinks, champagne, all the normal stuff.

## 4 Leisure & The Arts

### A. AT THE 5-SCREEN CINEMA

*Use the clues to complete the word puzzle and find the hidden word.*

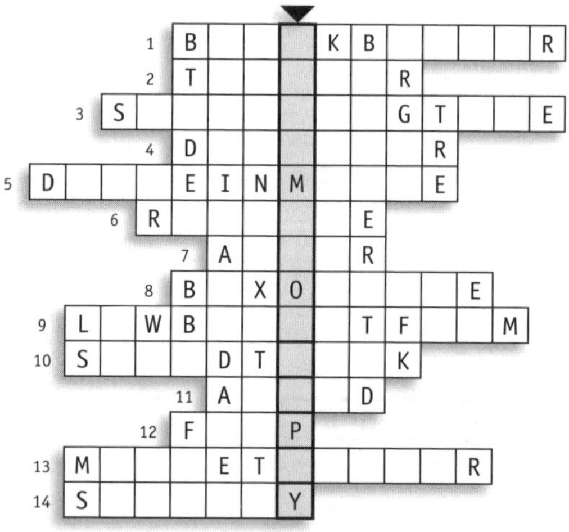


**1.** A well-known film which makes a lot of money.
**2.** A short filmed advert for a movie.
**3.** The time the film lasts on the screen.
**4.** The person who directs the film.
**5.** A movie you can go to in your car.
**6.** When a new film is made available to the public.
**7.** The person who acts.
**8.** Where you buy tickets for the cinema or theatre.
**9.** A motion picture which is shot on a low budget.
**10.** The sound recording of the film.
**11.** A brilliant actor / actress / terrific film.
is nominated for a prize.
**12.** A movie which doesn't make a hit.
**13.** Another word for a cinema.
**14.** The background to where the story takes place.
**Hidden word:** The art of film-making.

## B. A FULL-LENGTH FILM OR A SHORT FEATURE

***Add vowels to find the kind of film described.***

1. A film with no voices: S__L__NT M__V__ __
2. A dramatic film: DR__M__
3. A film which imagines the future: SC__ __NC__ F__CT__ __N
4. A Far West film: W__ST__RN
5. A film to frighten you: H__RR__R
6. A film where things happen all the time: __CT__ __N
7. A movie with lots of songs: M__S__C__L
8. A film full of adventure: __DV__NT__R__
9. An amusing movie: C__M__DY
10. A film which talks about the past: H__ST__R__C__L
11. A series of images or computer graphics: C__RT__ __N
12. A film about people fighting with guns etc. : W__R

## C. THEATRE & SHOWS

***Are the comments true or false?***

There was a full house on the opening night. The audience was waiting with bated breath. Then the curtain went up, the lights went on, and the stage came to life.
The play was tremendous. The scenery was magical. There was an awkward silence when one of the actresses forgot her lines in act one and had to be given a cue, however the momentum was never lost.
During the interval, the playgoers were lucky enough to meet with the backers and the script-writer.
The punch line was met with a round of applause.
The whole cast appeared together after the play to receive enthusiastic applause.
All the critics agreed – the show was a triumph.
Later that night, when the theatre was deserted, I was lucky enough to speak to the leading lady.
"We rehearsed like mad", she said. "Yesterday we all acted so badly. It just goes to show – A bad dress rehearsal means a good performance."

1. The article is about a ballet. ....................
2. The theatre was empty. ....................
3. Anticipation was high. ....................
4. There was a magician on scene. ....................
5. The actress clean forgot her words. ....................
6. The person who wrote the play and the patrons talked to the audience. ....................
7. The crowning touch to the play was a flop. ....................
8. The audience booed at the end of the play. ....................

## D. EXHIBITIONS AND MUSEUMS

*Choose the right answer.*

**1.** The person who runs the museum is the:
**a)** Curator **b)** Caretaker

**2.** Someone who gives works of art to a museum is a:
**a)** Donor **b)** Donator

**3.** A benefactor of the art world is a:
**a)** Benefit of the arts **b)** Patron of the arts

**4.** A structure of historical importance is a:
**a)** Monument **b)** Monumentum

**5.** An assembly of works of art, which is always on show, is a:
**a)** Permanent collection **b)** Constant collection

**6.** Someone who collects works of art is a:
**a)** Collection **b)** Collector

**7.** The art of putting works of art back into a good condition is to:
**a)** Restore **b)** Recondition

**8.** Something on display for the public to see is an:
**a)** Exhibitor **b)** Exhibit

**9.** To go into a museum you pay an:
**a)** Entrance fee **b)** Entrance rate

**10.** Something which has been lent to the museum is:
**a)** On loan **b)** On lent

**11.** Something which has been left to the museum is:
**a)** An inquest **b)** A bequest

**12.** A hand-made object of archaeological interest, usually to be used as a tool is:
**a)** An artefact **b)** An artfact

## E. FICTIONAL AND NON-FICTIONAL LITERATURE

↘ ***Find 10 kinds of written work in the word snake.***

shortstoryautobiographyessayspoetryjournalprosenovelmythdiary folktalebiography

...................................................................................................................

...................................................................................................................

## F. A GOOD READ

↘ ***Is the critic being critical (-) or complimentary (+)?***

**1.** Works by this popular author are consistently good reading.
**2.** I don't like to criticize but it's amazing he ever got published!
**3.** That's definitely the best title anyone has come up with for ages.
**4.** Not only is the plot disappointing but the writer thinks he's funny.
**5.** It must have been a feat of endurance to find a publisher for this one.
**6.** It's wonderful to see that an inexperienced agent can pick out a bestseller.
**7.** The repetitiveness in the blurb on the back of the book is enough to put anyone off.
**8.** Frankly, I'm not surprised he received 20 rejection slips before the book was accepted.
**9.** It must be the best bookstore I've ever browsed around.
**10.** If the cover and the spine are anything to go by, give this one a miss.
**11.** If you need a proficient printer you don't need to look any further.
**12.** That author is worth his weight in gold – I hope he gets good royalties!

## G. CAN YOU PLAY MUSIC BY EAR?

↘ ***Put a word into the gap.***

- amateur
- jazz
- latecomers
- musicians
- choir
- conductor
- concert
- orchestra
- festival
- classical

We went to the most wonderful **1)** __________ last night. There was a full **2)** ____________ with violins, trumpets, bassoons – everything! The **3)** _____________ was standing at the front with his baton, back to us, directing the **4)** __________ in the pit, and dressed in black tie with tails. On top of which there was a **5)** ___________ of 40 singers – all dressed in black and white. I didn't think I would like **6)** ___________ music - but I'm certainly a convert now!
There was only one drawback – Tom and Jerry missed the first half because they arrived late, and there was a big sign saying "Doors closed – **7)** ___________ will not be allowed in" – they had to wait until the interval.
Well, I'm afraid that I prefer going to listen to a **8)** ___________ band – in fact, I'm going to a music **9)** ___________ next month – would you like to come?
Thanks - I'd love to – I really enjoy listening to **10)** ____________ performers before they get to be famous!

## H. POP MUSIC – FAME AT LAST!

***Match the remark (1-6) to the response (A-F).***

**1.** I need somewhere to record my new hit.

**2.** Who's that really cool star over there?

**3.** Who are all those people standing in line?

**4.** I've been told that their latest hit topped the charts.

**5.** They've got a great repertoire on the CD which came out last month.

**6.** I've got all their recordings – I must see them when they are on tour – they might even come to our town!

**A.** They're the fans – they've been waiting here all night just to get a glimpse of her!

**B.** We tend to get more gigs than big concerts in a place like this!

**C.** There's a great new recording studio in Mere Street.

**D.** I think the group even got a gold disk for their latest compilation.

**E.** He's a pop singer – he records with the Boo Hoo band.

**F.** I like the 5th track best – the love song of course!

## I. AT THE MATCH

***Match the word on the left to a definition on the right.***

**1.** Stadium • • **A.** Playing field for sports like football and rugby
**2.** Pitch • • **B.** A place for playing tennis or squash, for example
**3.** Court • • **C.** A sports ground with tiers of seats for those watching

**4.** Referee • • **D.** The person who makes sure the rules are obeyed, for example, in a tennis match
**5.** Umpire • • **E.** The arbitrator in a football or boxing match

**6.** Captain • • **F.** A group of people who play together
**7.** Team • • **G.** A person who competes in a game
**8.** Opponent • • **H.** The head of the team
**9.** Player • • **I.** The person you play against

**10.** Spectator • • **J.** A follower of a certain team
**11.** Supporter • • **K.** The person who watches a game

12. Beat • • **L.** To be victorious
13. Win • • **M.** To be defeated
14. Lose • • **N.** To gain points in a game
15. Score • • **O.** To do better than

## J. A TRIP TO THE ZOO WITH THE FAMILY

↘ ***Complete the text with the following words.***

• niece and nephew • grandmother and grandfather • twin • half brother • father-in-law • step-mother • great uncle's • grandchildren

Dear Joy,
You can't imagine what a remarkable day we had last Tuesday when the whole family went to the zoo – just except you to my great regret – my dear **(1)** person born at the same time as me .............................. It was a celebration for our **(2)** mother's uncle's .............................. 100th birthday – quite an event! He was so happy when he unwrapped all his presents.
Of course the elderly relations were all there – our **(3)** father's mother and father ............................, and all of our cousins. It did occur to me that some of the animals in the cages looked rather like our **(4)** father's second wife ....................................... - no, I mustn't be unkind! Luckily our father and his wife had decided not to bring our **(5)** the child they had during their second marriage ........................................!! He is a spoilt brat!
All the **(6)** children of my children ........................................ran around the spacious wild animal park (without getting eaten by a lion or tiger, so no-one needed rescuing thankfully!). Luckily, my **(7)** brother's daughter and son ....................................... were there to keep an eye on everyone. **(8)** My husband's father ....................................... even rode on a camel!
Well, I must dash - B2W & ATB

## K. ONE WORD – MANY MEANINGS!

↘ ***Put the same word into all the sentences in each group. You may need to conjugate the verb.***

Miss / Plant / Tip / Issue / Launch / Quote / Meet

**1.** Could you __________ us for 200 units?
Could you __________ the item number?
Could you __________ what your boss actually said?

**2.** This is __________ 6 of the new trade magazine.
They will __________ new shares next month.
The __________ in question, is how much to invest in the new machines.
Please don't make an __________ out of this!

**3.** Pleased to __________ you.
__________ a deadline.
__________ customer requirements.

→

→ **4.** The __________ is located in the Butterfly Industrial Estate.
We have to make an inventory of the __________ to transfer to the Manchester factory.
Could you put that __________ in the corner of your office?

**5.** Could you put that rubbish on the __________________?
How much should we leave as a _________________ in the restaurant?
That's a good idea – a really useful ______________________!!!

**6.** The Titanic was __________________ in 1911.
We are going to ____________________ our new product on the market in February.
I think we are ready to __________________ production.

**7.** Oh no, we're late. We're going to ________________ our train!
I don't think you understand. You have _______________ the point.
He was such a nice chap, our manager. Now he's gone, we really ______________ him.

## L. HIGH DAYS AND HOLIDAYS

↘ ***Look at the 2 charts and answer the questions.***

**AMERICAN FEDERAL HOLIDAYS (2010)**

| | |
|---|---|
| Friday, January 1st | New Year's Day |
| Monday, January 18th* | Birthday of Martin Luther King, Jr. |
| Monday, February 15th* | Washington's Birthday |
| Monday, May 31st | Memorial Day |
| Monday, July 5th | Independence Day |
| Monday, September 16th | Labor Day |
| Monday, October 11th* | Columbus Day |
| Thursday, November 11th* | Veterans Day |
| Thursday, November 25th | Thanksgiving Day |
| Friday, December 24th | Christmas Day |

If the Federal holiday falls on a Saturday, it will be replaced by the Friday before, and if it falls on a Sunday, it will be replaced by the Friday before.
July 4th (Independence Day) and December 25th (Christmas Day) fall on a weekend, so July 5th will be treated as a Federal holiday for the former, and December 24th for the latter.
*Some busines may choose to stay open on these days.

**UK PUBLIC HOLIDAYS (2010)**

| | | |
|---|---|---|
| Friday, January 1st | New Year's Day | Everywhere |
| Monday, January 4th | 2nd January | Scotland |
| Wednesday, March 17th | Saint Patrick's Day | Ireland |
| Friday, April 2nd | Good Friday | Everywhere |
| Monday, April 5th | Easter Monday | England, Ireland, Wales |
| Tuesday, April 6th | Easter Tuesday | Ireland |
| Monday, May 3rd | May Day Holiday | Everywhere |
| Monday, May 17th | Victoria Day | Scotland |
| Monday, May 31st | Spring Bank Holiday | Everywhere |
| Monday, July 12th | Orangeman's Day | Ireland |
| Monday, August 2nd | Summer Bank Holiday | Scotland |
| Monday, August 30th | Summer Bank Holiday | England, Ireland, Wales |
| Monday, December 27th* | Christmas Day | Everywhere |
| Tuesday, December 28th* | Boxing Day | Everywhere |

*Because December 25th and December 26th fall on a weekend

**1.** Do the UK and the USA have the same public holiday system?

..................................................................................................................................

**2.** Do the same rules apply if the public holiday is at the weekend?

..................................................................................................................................

**3.** Do the English people and the Americans have the same number of bank holidays?

..................................................................................................................................

**4.** Do both countries have a national day?

..................................................................................................................................

**5.** Are there some public holidays both countries have in common?

..................................................................................................................................

**6.** In America, is every Federal holiday a compulsory day off?

..................................................................................................................................

**7.** Are there any public holidays in the middle of the week?

..................................................................................................................................

**8.** Do the four countries which make up the United Kingdom always have the same bank holidays?

..................................................................................................................................

## JUST A WARM UP TO THE GRAMMAR SECTION

↘ *Can you correct the following common (grammatical or lexical) mistake(s)?*

**1.** I must to call that famous explorer this afternoon.
**2.** I am agree.
**3.** How is Mary? She is attractive and bright.
**4.** How much time do you take to go to work?
**5.** He was much fatter there is 10 years ago.
**6.** I look forward to hear from you.
**7.** She is responsible of quality.
**8.** The economical situation is not very good.
**9.** He works all the day all days of the week.
**10.** We are interested by your proposal.
**11.** I want that you pay attention.
**12.** In the first time, we'll look at the pie chart.
**13.** I would like some informations about...
**14.** It's high time you speak fluent English!
**15.** You don't must touch that handle!
**16.** One of the manager has forgotten his laptop.
**17.** It exists people who have no ambition.
**18.** I'd rather you use the other phone.
**19.** Never I have seen such an efficient production line.
**20.** Nowhere are people such hardworking as in our company, there is so a lot to do!

***Voici quelques exemples des erreurs fréquemment commises en anglais.***
***Pour vous aider à les éviter, nous vous proposons, sur le site Internet www.nathan.fr/toeic :***
***- des fiches des principaux points de grammaire à connaître***
***- de nombreux exercices d'application.***

***Vous pourrez ainsi déceler vos « faiblesses » en grammaire, et les résoudre rapidement !***

# Answer Section

# Answer Section

## The company

### 1. Types of Business

**A. What kind of Business?**: 1. k, 2. e, 3. c, 4. j, 5. f, 6. a, 7. i, 8. h, 9. d, 10. g, 11. b, 12. l

**B. Which Business Sector?**

| | | | | | | | | | | | | | | | | | | | | | | | | | | | | | |
|---|---|---|---|---|---|---|---|---|---|---|---|---|---|---|---|---|---|---|---|---|---|---|---|---|---|---|---|---|---|
| | | | | M | | | | T | E | X | T | I | L | E | | | | | | | | | | | | | | | A |
| C | H | E | M | I | C | A | L | S | | | | N | | | | | | | | | | | | B | | | | | E |
| | | L | | N | | | | | | | | D | | | P | A | C | K | I | N | G | P | L | A | N | T | | | R |
| | | E | | I | | | | | | | | U | | | S | | | | | | | | | N | | | | | O |
| | | C | | N | | | T | | | | | S | | A | U | T | O | M | O | T | I | V | E | K | | | | | S |
| P | | T | | G | | | R | | | | | T | L | | S | | | | | | | | | I | | | | | P |
| U | | R | | | | | A | | | | | R | O | | T | | | | | | | | | N | | | | | A |
| B | I | O | T | E | C | H | N | O | L | O | G | Y | G | | A | M | E | T | A | L | L | U | R | G | Y | | | | C |
| L | | N | | | | | S | | | | | | I | | I | | | | | | | | | & | | | | | E |
| I | | I | | | | | P | | | | | | S | | N | | | | | | | | | F | | | | | M |
| S | | C | | | | | O | | | | | | T | M | A | N | U | F | A | C | T | U | R | I | N | G | | | A |
| H | | S | | | | | R | | | | | | I | | B | | | | | | | | | N | | | A | | R |
| I | | & | | | | | T | | | | | | C | | L | | | | | | | | | A | | | G | | I |
| N | | I | | | M | A | T | E | R | I | A | L | S | & | E | N | G | I | N | E | E | R | I | N | G | | R | | N |
| G | | T | | | | | | | | | | | P | | D | | | | | | | | | C | | | I | | E |
| | | S | | | | | | | | | | | L | | E | | | | | | | | | I | | | C | | & |
| | | E | | | | | | | | | | | A | | V | | | | | | | | | A | | | U | | D |
| | | R | | | T | | | | | | F | | T | | E | | | | B | | | | | L | | | L | | E |
| E | N | V | I | R | O | N | M | E | N | T | A | L | F | | L | | | | R | | | | | S | | | T | | F |
| | | I | N | D | U | S | T | R | I | E | S | | O | | O | | | | O | | | | L | E | I | S | U | R | E |
| | | C | H | A | R | I | T | Y | | | H | | R | | P | | | | A | | | | | R | | | R | | N |
| | | E | | | I | | A | | | | I | | M | | M | | | | D | | | | | V | | | E | | C |
| | | S | | | S | | V | | | | O | | | | E | | | | C | | | | | I | | | | | E |
| | | | R | | M | | I | | | | N | | | | N | | | | A | | | | | C | | | | | |
| | | T | E | L | E | C | O | M | M | U | N | I | C | A | T | I | O | N | S | | | | | E | | | | | |
| | | | T | | | | N | | | | | | | | | | | | T | | | | | S | | | | | |
| | | | A | | | | I | | | | | | | | | | | | I | | | | | | | | | | |
| | | | I | | | | C | O | N | S | T | R | U | C | T | I | O | N | N | | | | | | | | | | |
| | | | L | | | | S | | | | | | | | | | | | G | | | | | | | | | | |
| P | H | A | R | M | A | C | E | U | T | I | C | A | L | & | H | E | A | L | T | H | C | A | R | E | | | | | |

### 2. Company Structure

**A Multinational Company:** a) Parent company, b) Turnover, c) Subsidiary, d) Sister company, e) Overseas branch, f) B.U. Business Unit (SBU Strategic Business Unit) / Division, g) Department, h) Head office, i) Shareholder

### 3. Company History

**A. Business is booming:** 1. founder, 2. set up, 3. based in, 4. core business, 5. forward planning, 6. incorporate, 7. Memorandum and articles of association, 8. location, 9. premises, 10. in-house, 11. merger, 12. growth, 13. share capital, 14. turnover, 15. competitors, 16. ranks, 17. market share, 18. partnership, 19. joint management, 20. takeover, 21. buyout, 22. go public, 23. company policy, 24. company image

**B. 6 Horrible Homonyms:** 1. Affect (verb) / effect (noun), 2. Billed / build, 3. Sell / cell, 4. Cent / sent / cent, 5. Complement / compliment, 6. Council / Counsel

**C. The Rise and Fall of the Company**
ORGANISATIONAL CHANGES: 1. Restructure, 2. Cutbacks, 3. Upgrade, 4. Downsize, 5. Phase in (or out), 6. Build up, 7. Streamline, 8. Strengthen, 9. Tighten up (tighten your belt), 10. Update
DOWNHILL: 11. Downward trend, 12. Sharp fall, 13. Steady decrease, 14. Weakening
SKYWARD: 15. Constant rise, 16. Dramatic increase, 17. General improvement, 18. Marked progress, 19. Upward trend, 20. Move forward

## 4. All Kinds of Jobs

**A. Are you an odd-job man?: a: Across:** 1. Surgeon, 2. Physiotherapist, 3. Doctor (G.P. = General Practitioner). **Down:** 4. Social Worker, 5. Nurse, 6. Pharmacist (Chemist UK). **b. Across:** 1. Financial Analyst, 2. Accountant, 3. Book Keeper. **Down:** 4. Auditor, 5; judge, 6. Lawyer (can include: attornay, counsellor, solicitor, barrister ...) 7. Treasurer. **c. Across:** 1. Police officer, 2. Nightwatcher, 3. Fire Fighter (Fireman, UK), 4. Caretaker. **Down:** 5. Civil Servant. **d. Across:** 1. Sustainable Energy Expert, 2. Farmer, 3. Carpenter, 4. Builder **Down:** 5. Electrician, 6. Plumber. **e. Across:** 1. Translator, 2. Coach, 3. Author, 4. Photographer, 5. Musician, 6. Singer, 7. Librarian (Att.: the difference between a library where you borrow a book and a bookshop where you buy a book!) **Down:** 8. Reporter, 9. Teacher, 10 Actor, 11. Architect. **f. Accross:** 1. Project Leader, 2. Purchaser, 3. Door-to-door salesman, 4. Manufacturer. **Down:** 5. (machine) Operative, 6. PRO, 7. Clerk, 8. Engineer.
**B. An Organizational Chart (UK Organisation Chart):** 1. Chairman and C.E.O. – Chief Executive Officer (UK: Managing Director), 2. Senior Vice President (Corporate Development), 3. Senior Vice President (Manufacturing) (UK: Director), 4. Chief Financial Officer, 5. Chief Information Officer (UK: Public Relations Officer / Manager), 6. Vice President (Sales and Business Development), 7. V.P. (Product Management) (UK: Director), 8. General Manager, 9. V.P. Human Resources, 10. Chief Accountant, 11. Strategic Partner Sales, 12. Strategic Partner Marketing, 13. Production Director, 14. R&D Director (UK: Manager), 15. Export Sales Manager, 16. Domestic Sales Manager, 17. Workshop Manager, 18. Assembly Foreman, 19. Purchaser, 20. Quality Manager, 21. EH&S Manager.
**C. Who reports to whom?:** 1. in charge of, 2. reports to, 3. is accountable to, 4. assists, 5. oversees, 6. assisted by, 7. responsible to, 8. responsible for
**D. Your position in the company:** 1. Senior executive, 2. Junior executive (Also: Senior and Junior Partner, for example, in a law firm), 3. Colleague, 4. Head, 5. Self-employed, 6. Trainee, 7. Supervisor, 8. Skilled worker, 9. Unskilled worker (Semi-skilled workers have some skills but not enough to do specialized work), 10. Temporary worker (temp), 11. Seasonal worker, 12. Out worker, 13. Guest worker, 14. Moonlighter, 15. Casual worker, 16. Apprentice.

## 5. The Working Day

**A. It's all in a day's work:** 1C Public Holiday (UK: Bank holiday), 2A Maternity Leave, 3D Sick Leave, 4B Day off, 5E Paid holiday (Paid leave).
Working hours: 1C Clock in (punch in / sign in), 2H Knock off, 3A Full-Time, 4G Office Hours, 5D Flexi time, 6I Part-Time, 7B Clock Out (Clock off / Sign off), 8J Time Clock (time card), 9F Take a break, 10E Work Day (Working Day / Business Day).
We are very Busy: 1D 24/7, 2C Overtime, 3A Night Shift, 4B Unsocial hours.
A busman's holiday is a holiday where you do the same things as at work.

## 6. On the Premises

**A. Optimizing Plant layout:** 1. Caretaker's lodge, 2. Delivery Area (Receiving) (or Delivery Bay), 3. Sick Room, 4. Staff Canteen, 5. Workshops, 6. Rest Area, 7. Production Line, 8. Toilets (Ladies, Gents, Rest Rooms, Loo), 9. Assembly Line, 10. Meeting Room, 11. Quality Control, 12. Packaging & Warehousing, 13. Dispatch / Shipping, 14. Administration offices, 15. Reception, 16. Car Park.
**B. Could you tidy up your office?!:** 1. Calendar, 2. Chair, 3. Desk, 4. Desktop Computer, 5. Laptop Computer, 6. USB Flash Drive (USB Key), 7. File (Folder), 8. Drawer, 9. Stapler, 10. Ruler, 11. Cell Phone (UK: Mobile phone), 12. Palmtop Organiser, 13. Pencil, 14. Rubber, 15. Calculator, 16. Pen, 17. Waste Bin (UK: Waste Paper Basket / Bin), 18. Shredder, 19. Paper, 20. Bulletin Board

# Answer Section

## Administrative departments

### 1. Finance

**A. Are you good at numbers?:** 1. 1B (n.b. No "s" on hundred. The "and" is used in British English but not in American English), 2F, 3A, ("a" or "one") 4D, 5C, 6E

2. 1C, 2F (n.b. The "0" before the decimal point is said "nought", the "0" after the decimal point is said "oh". The figures after the decimal point are said individually), 3B, 4E, 5D, 6A

3. 1F, 2A, 3E, 4B (A ratio), 5C, 6D

4. 1D, 2F, 3C, 4A, 5B, 6E (n.b. $^1/_{10}$ = one-tenth, $^2/_{10}$ = two-tenths)

5. 1E (to add), 2A (to subtract / deduct), 3B (to divide), 4D (to multiply), 5F (or makes nineteen), 6C (or five point 6 recurring)

**B. Different kinds of accounting:** 1. Cost Accounting, 2. Auditing, 3. Creative Accounting, 4. Managerial Accounting (or Management Accounting), 5. Bookkeeping, 6. Tax Accounting

**C. In the accounts department:** 1. pay back (repay), 2. carry forward (also carry over), 3. mileage rate, 4. afford, 5. miscount, 6. expense account, 7. entry, 8. unpaid invoice, 9. I.O.U., 10. ledger, 11. incidental expenses (sundry expenses), 12. subsidize

**D. Invoicing and payment:** 1. Method of payment: Payment by instalments, Hire purchase, Prepaid 2. Payment terms: Payment date, Mid-July, Balance due / due date 3. Billing: Bill for services rendered, Invoice, Subtotal 4. Late payment: Overdue payment, Payment past due, Owe

**E. Financial Statements:** (1) Balance Sheet (2) Assets (3) Liabilities Note: Total Shareholder Equity can also be called Shareholder's Funds. Net Assets = stockholder equity minus intangible assets, e.g. goodwill and I.P. (Intellectual Property) (4) Income statement / Profit & Loss (P&L) / Statement of Operations (5) Revenue (Total Revenue / Gross Profit) (6) Operating Expenses (7) Net Income (Bottom Line) (8) Cash Flow Statement

**F. Corporate Finance:** Overheads – fixed costs: Running costs – operating expenses: Expenditure – outgoings: Man-hour – person hour: Miscellaneous expense – general expense: Forecast – prediction: YTD – Year-to-date (Cumulative over a certain period): Break-even point - Revenue = expenses (Point at which you can start to make a profit): Unit cost – production cost per unit item: Yield – Rate of return (on investment): Cost analysis – costing: Operating margin – Operating profit margin: Ready cash – cash in hand: Debt – arrears: Rate of Exchange – currency exchange rate: Cash flow – Cash inflow and outflow: Bankruptcy (to go bankrupt) – insolvency (to be insolvent): Liquidate (to go into liquidation) – Wind up (down) / close down: To show a loss – To show a shortfall

SWOT: Strength – Weakness – Opportunities – Threats. By the way, a "swot" is also someone who works or studies hard!

**G. Taxation:** 1a), 2c), 3a), 4b), 5c), 6b) Also called Goods and Services Tax, 7a) or IRS (UK - Inland Revenue), 8b), 9c) (UK- Tax Year), 10a), 11c), 12b), 13a), 14 c), 15b) (Pay as you earn)

### 2. Human Resources

**A. Remuneration:** 1. Perk, 2. Overtime, 3. Payroll Costs, 4. Profit sharing, 5. Bonus, 6. Pay rise, 7. Take-home pay, 8. Wage / salary, 9. Lunch(eon) voucher, 10. Incentive plan, 11. Fringe Benefits, 12. Payday, 13. Weekly pay packet, 14. Stock Options, 15. Work sharing, 16. Earn, 17. Pension Plan, 18. Payslip, 19. Award, 20. Double time. (Also: time and a half) Down: Performance Appraisal

**B. Situations vacant:** 1. Goes to job centre, 2. Writes up resumé (C.V.), 3. Looks at job adverts (advertisements, ads), 4. Fills in application form, 5. Writes cover letter (UK Covering letter), 6. Applies for job, 7. Goes through screening process, 8a. Yes – (Candidate) Put on short list. 8b. No – (Candidate) Put on waiting list, 9. Has interview, 10a. Appointed for the job, 10b. Turned down for the job, 11. Has a 3-month trial period (or Probationary period), 12. Gives permanent part-time contract.

**C. Classified Ads:** hiring – applicant – hands-on experience – hard worker – recruiting – experienced – basic salary – responsibilities – qualified – skills – candidate – motivated team – working knowledge – per annum – vacancy – drive – work permit – background – qualifications

**D. You've got the job:**

Dear Ms. Hopeful,

Thank you for coming to the interview in Los Angeles last week. We would like to offer you the position of Junior Consultant, commencing 25th January 2011. You will have a statutory 6-month probationary period followed by a permanent full-time contract.

The rewards package includes a starting salary of $5,050 per month, to be increased according to your proficiency level. You will also be paid commission on a percentage basis according to the contracts signed, and there is a payment by results scheme which enables you and your future colleagues to increase their monthly revenue.
The contracted hours of work are the equivalent of 10 hours a day multiplied by the number of working days in the month. Your leave entitlement (or paid leave) of 2 days a calendar month will accumulate as from your starting date.
Because you will be moving to the States, we shall provide a relocation allowance.
Career prospects and advancement are encouraged and we shall help you on the path to success with in-house training and computer-based training programs.
Please find enclosed a job description and the terms and conditions of employment, as well as the agreement for you to return signed.
Should you require any further information, please do not hesitate to contact my office.
Yours sincerely,
James Joboffer,
H.R. Manager

**E. Leaving or losing a job:** 1. Redundancy plan, 2. $500,000 Golden Handshake for C.E.O., 3. Sacked for Professional Misconduct, 4. No more merit bonuses. Note: To give notice = to hand in notice. To sack = to fire = to dismiss. To lay off – to be laid off. To be unemployed = to be on gardening leave = to be on furlough

**F. Labour relations:** 1. Short time working, 2. Unfair dismissal, 3. Bullying, 4. Sexual harassment, 5. Understaffed, 6. Minimum wage, 7. Grievance, 8. Dispute, 9. Trouble-maker, 10. Worker representation, 11. Strike, 12. Picket line, 13. Scab, 14. Walk-out, 15. In company time, 16. Absenteeism, 17. Arbitrate (Arbitrator), 18. Labor Union (UK: Trade union), 19. Works council (Works committee), 20. Labor code, 21. Collective bargaining

## 3. I.T.

**A. Computer keywords:** 1C, 2F, 3G, 4A, 5D, 6E, 7B

**B. Hardware:** 1. Scanner, 2. USB, 3. Screen, 4. CD Drive, 5. Printer, 6. Mouse, 7. CPU, 8. Keyboard

**C. Software:** 1) Computer memory, 2) Data, 3) Computer programs, 4) Bits / Bytes / Megabytes / Gigabytes, 5) Operating system, 6) Computer games, 7) Driver software, 8) Media player, 9) Database management; Word processing; Desk top publishing; Presentation software, 10) Educational software

**D. Surfing the web:** 1.A, 2E, 3.H, 4.L, 5.F, 6.I, 7.D, 8.K, 9.B, 10.G, 11.J, 12.C

**E. Computer problems:** 1.b, 2.e, 3.f, 4.a, 5.c, 6.d

**F. I had no Internet connection:** 1. I needed High Speed Internet Access, 2. I wanted to use my WIFI but was to far away from the AP to use Wireless, 3. I had to use an Ethernet Cable, 4. Which I plugged into a wall jack, 5. This had no effect, so I had to re-boot my computer, 6. In fact another program was a bandwidth hog and disrupted my connection, 7. Conclusion: Beware of P2P applications!

**G. 5 Confusing words:** 1. Actually / currently, 2. Advised / advice, 3. Ensure / insure / assure, 4. Check / inspected / control, 5. Besides / beside

## 4. Logistics

**A. In the warehouse:**

**reception / incoming goods:** Check the raw materials / part assemblies / purchased parts, on arrival from the supplier / sub-contractor – Sign the delivery note

**warehouse / storehouse / storeroom / stockroom:** Unload / unpack the goods – Use a fork – lift truck / hand pallet truck to handle the goods – Stack the raw materials / part assemblies / purchased parts/ finished products on the rack

**dispatch / shipping:** Make up the order and package the goods – Dispatch the finished product – Deliver the goods to the customer

**B. Stock Management:** – Calculate the lead time – Check the delivery deadlines – Warn customer of a delivery delay
Use FIFO Management tools – Take stock to avoid a shortage / lack of goods – Check the stock-in-hand
Send a reminder to the supplier about the remainder of the order – Re-order goods before being out of stock
Update your stocklist (U.K.) / inventory (U.S.A.) – Once a month / year, do the inventory / stocktaking

**C. What's on the sticker?:** Expiry date – Handle with care – Hazardous materials – RFID tag – Quality control Label – Barcode – Batch number

**D. Freight Transportation:** CARRIAGE COSTS – Haulier Freight rate – Carrier Loading charges – Haulage company handling charges
PAPERWORK – Consignment note – Certificate of origin – Air waybill – Shipment notice – Freight forwarder invoice – Customs clearance documents – Packing list
CUSTOMS – Regulations – Duty – Border - Bonded warehouse – Goods in bond – Prohibited goods

**E. Goods in transit**
Lorry (UK) – Truck (USA)

# Answer Section

Delivery van – HGV (heavy goods vehicle)
FCL (Full container load) – Part load
Rail transport – Carriage by sea
Driver (UK) – Trucker (USA)
Trailer – RORO (roll on roll off)
Cubic capacity – Net weight
Time of arrival – Scheduled time of departure

## 5. Maintenance

**A. What a week!**

We have had a lot of problems recently. Just take a look at this report:

Monday: Electricity – we had a power cut so there was no power supply to the machines.

Tuesday: Several machine breakdowns. We had to put "out of order" signs up on them all – and just before a customer audit! The sudden failure (quite unexpected) of the punching machine caused the most downtime, when the operators had to sit around doing nothing while the equipment was out of use.

Wednesday: Time to sort out the reasons for machine failure. This is what we found:

Wear – some parts had just been progressively worn away.

Neglect – some of the machines had not been looked after well enough.

Core damage – we cannot repair the material and will need to order new parts.

Thursday: Electricity overload – this time too much energy! There seems to be an anomaly in the system, something is not quite right.

You can just imagine the backlog we have now – really late compared with our schedule!

Friday: T.G.I.F. If there is a malfunction over the weekend, someone else will have to mend it. (TGIF = Thank God it's Friday!)

**B. Prevention is better than cure:** 1. recondition, 2. refit, 3. after sales service, 4. bench marking, 5. repair, 6. do it now, 7. shut down, 8. overhaul, 9. FMECA. Hidden word: dismantle.

## 6. Management

**A. Business Planning:** 1. Goal – target – aim, 2. First quarter, 3. Second half / semester, 4. Outcome, 5. Guidelines, 6. Forecast, 7. In the short / medium / long run, 8. Compulsory, 9. Corporate strategy, 10. Profitability, 11. Cost effective, 12. anticipate

Speech: Forecast – quarter – target – cost effective – half - productivity – guidelines – compulsory – corporate strategy – anticipate – long run

**B. An over-paid manager:** 1. workload, 2. paperwork, 3. business sense, 4. wavelength, 5. involved, 6. masterminds, 7. feedback, 8. corporate strategy, 9. need-to-know, 10. businesslike, 11. adaptability, 12. overworked & underpaid

**C. Running a company:** 1. MBO, 2. Teamwork, 3. Leadership, 4. Mediate, 5. Goodwill, 6. Ideas box, 7. Tackle a problem, 8. Be aware, 9. Sensitive issue, 10. The pros and cons, 11. Shortfall in earnings, 12. Fall short of forecasts

**D. Corporate Governance and Ethics:** 1. Truthful, 2. Fair, 3. Honest, 4. Decent, 5. Moral, 6. Legal, 7. Respect, responsibility, results, 8. Environmental responsibility, 9. Fairness towards employees, 10. Accountability to local communities, 11. Providing responsible products and services to customers, 12. Maintaining a healthy rate of return for investors

## 7. EH&S

**A. Safety first:** 1a), 2a), 3a), 4b), 5a), 6b), 7b), 8a), 9b), 10b), 11b), 12a), 13b), 14b), 15a).

NB: Flammable and inflammable mean the same thing. Non-flammable means the item cannot be fired.

# *The product*

## 1. Marketing & Advertising

**A. The marketing mix:** Product – Price – Place – Promotion

**B. A marketing brief:** 1. Marketing brief, 2. A non-starter, 3. Product range, 4. Market trend, 5. Target market, 6. Opinion poll, 7. Market research, 8. OTS – Opportunity to see, 9. Brand awareness, 10. Eye-catching packaging, 11. Jingle, 12. Launch

**C. Which word should I use?** 1.D, 2.R, 3.G, 4.N, 5.Q, 6.B, 7.J, 8.H, 9.E, 10.L, 11.A, 12.M, 13.I, 14.P, 15.F, 16.C, 17.K, 18.O

**D. Different kinds of promotion & advertising:** 1.E, 2.I, 3.B, 4.L, 5.G, 6.D, 7.K, 8.A, 9.H, 10.J, 11.C, 12.F

**E. Let's give sales a boost:** 1. Showcase, 2. Blurb, 3. Advertising, 4. Advertiser, 5. Media Coverage, 6. Prime Time, 7. Viewership, 8. Teaser campaign, 9. Display case, 10. Showroom, 11. Brand loyalty, 12. Loyalty card, 13. Booklet, 14. Promotion, 15. Copy

## 2. Products

**A. Product Features in all shapes and sizes:** 1. Throw-away, 2. Fake, 3. Shoddy, 4. Produce, 5. Custom-made, custom-built, tailor-made, 6. Cordless, 7. Own brand label, 8. Good value for money, 9. Foodstuffs, 10. Sell-by date, 11. Taken the place of, 12. Watertight (étanche à l'eau), airtight (étanche à l'air), tamper-proof, refillable, self-locking, 13. Lid, 14. Lifespan, 15. No-brand articles.

**B. The bare necessities:** A: 1c, 2b, 3a. B: 1b, 2a. C: 1a, 2b. D: 1b, 2a. E: 1a, 2b. F: 1b, 2a. G: 1b, 2a.

C. 6 more confusing words: 1. Underside /downside, 2. Hardly / hard, 3. Lay down / lie down, 4. Rise / raise, 5. Remind / remember, 6. Earns / won

## 3. Production

**A. On the factory floor:**

Procedures: J.I.T.P. (Just in time production), self-inspection, process costing, lean production, safety instructions – People: foreman, mechanic, setter, workmate – Places: workshop, cleanroom, changing room, restricted area, rework area for defective products or customization – Problems: backlog, bottleneck, stoppage, wastage

**B. A production process flowchart:** 1. Purchase raw materials and purchased parts (outsourced / sub-contracted), 2. Prepare machine tools / tooling, 3. Do pilot / test run, 4. Prepare Product Schedule / planning / routing, 5. Write up work orders and standard work, 6. Initiate launch / product run, 7. Make as many by-products as possible, 8. Keep waste and scrap to a minimum, 9. Continue, 10. Better do Value Stream Mapping!, 11. Deliver part assemblies / subsets / semi-processed goods to the assembly line, 12. Work in progress / work in hand, 13. Smooth assembly process with no idle capacity time, 14. Shrink-wrap goods before dispatch

**C. A few more homonyms:** 1. Fax /facts, 2. Least / leased, 3. Principle /principal, 4. Right / write, 5. Stationery /stationary, 6. Bye /by /buy

## 4. Purchasing & Procurement

**A. Purchasing and procurement:** 1. Large red lights 2. 5 Euros 3. 01/03/20.. 4. 01/04/20.. 5. No – only 3 out of 5 boxes 6. 5.6 kg 7. Take-it-away Bros., 8. Fragile goods needing bubble wrap, 9. Within 30 days after delivery, 10. To Illuminated Interiors

**B. Purchasing parts:** 1.c, 2m, 3.k, 4.o, 5.n, 6.b, 7. d / I, 8. i / d, 9.e, 10.l, 11.h, 12.a, 13.j, 14.g, 15.f

**C. Some parts are lacking:** 1.B, 2.D, 3.F, 4.E, 5.A, 6.C

**D. Try your hand at...:** 1. Shortly / briefly, 2. Illegible / eligible, 3. Looking over / overlooked, 4. Personal / personnel

## 5. Quality

**A. The 5s:** sort, set in order / store, shine, standardize, sustain

**B. Quality catchwords:** Performance, Appearance, Reliability, Durability, Serviceability, Traceability

**C. The quality department:** One role of the quality department is to HANDLE COMPLAINTS when an item is not CONFORM. When you find a DEFECT you should take CORRECTIVE ACTION immediately, so that you continue to MEET CUSTOMER REQUIREMENTS and obtain a CERTIFICATE OF COMPLIANCE. You can either REPAIR, REPLACE, REWORK or RE-DESIGN the items. The goods which DEVIATE FROM THE NORM will have to be SCRAPPED. You may have to improve your TESTING PROCEDURES or alter the TOLERANCE.

Remember, PREVENTIVE ACTION will avoid NON-QUALITY COSTS and enable keeping customer GOODWILL. Of course, we are also responsible for certification, such as ISO.

**D. Zero defect?:** Shrinkage; Bad workmanship; Slapdash; Shoddy; Slipshod; Unreliable; Substandard; Wear & tear

## 6. Research, Development & Industrialization

**A. Advanced technology:**

- Technological awareness – keeping up to date with the latest technology; Technological lead – being a technological forerunner; Technological know-how – knowing how to do something; Technological gap – being rather behind in technology; – Leading-edge technology – the foremost position in a trend or technology; Out-of-date / outdated technology – old-fashioned technology; Obsolete technology – technology which is no longer applicable; High tech – the latest advancements in a certain technology; Rise of new technologies – the rapid development of new technology

- Experiment – a test under controlled conditions; Breakthrough – a major achievement in technology which enables further progress

Patent – government authorisation to an inventor for the sole use of the invention for a set time; (n.b. To patent) Patent pending – waiting to be protected by a government authorisation; Innovate – to begin or introduce something new

- Design lead time – the time between the initiation and the completion of a design process; Lean manufacturing – where storage, waste and errors are kept to a strict minimum; Unit costing – calculating the

cost of a given unit of a product
- Pilot study – a preliminary study; Prototype – an original, full-scale and working model of a new product; Sample – an example

**B. New technology buzzwords:** 1.c, 2.b, 3.b, 4.c, 5.a, 6.b.

**C. Equipment for the lab:** 1.d, 2.f, 3.i, 4.b, 5.n, 6.m, 7.k, 8.h, 9.a, 10.j, 11.e, 12.l, 13.c, 14.g

**D. Horrendous homonyms:** 1. Eight / ate, 2. Board / bored, 3. Foreword / forward, 4. Hear / here, 5. Meat / meet, 6. Piece / peace

**E. Bookworm specifications:** 1. 240 mm, 2. 180 mm, 3. 12 mm, 4. 0.65 kg, 5. 210 mm, 6. 25 mm, 7. 359 g, 8. 240 by 180 by 12, 9. 3045 $mm^2$, 10. 7612 $mm^3$

## 7. Sales & After Sales

**A. The retail trade – Where can you sell it?:** marketplace, department store, factory outlet, vending machine, bulk (wholesale) outlet, off-label store, supermarket, superstore, one-price store, convenience store, chain store, auction, shopping arcade / centre / mall, mail order business (MOB), the Internet, off-licence, retail outlet, cash & carry, self-service store

**B. What do you find in the shop?** 1. Sales person, 2. Floor / shop walker, 3. Reseller, 4. Tradesman, 5. Cashier, 6. Shelf-filler, 7. Shoplifter, 8. Fixtures and fittings, 9. Cash register, 10. Receipt, 11. Price tag, 12. Second-hand goods, 13. Display Unit, 14. Second-rate goods, 15. Shelving, 16. Check out

**C. Trading times:** Mass market / niche market ; Sunday trading / Weekday trading hours ; Stock clearance sale / Closing down sale ; Late night opening / Early closing hours ; Impulse buying / Planned purchase ; Returned goods / Refund request ; Retail / wholesale

**D. Trading trends :** a4; b1; c5; d2; e3

**E. Pricing and payment:** 1. Tax-inclusive price, 2. Grant a discount, 3. List price, 4. Knock-down prices, 5. Price cut, 6. Interest-free credit, 7. Instalment plan (UK Hire Purchase), 8. Charge account

**F. Corporate customers:** 1. Supplier, 2. Trade magazines (also "journal"), 3. Trade Fair (also "show", e.g. Car show, Boat Show, etc.), 4. Trademarks (also "Trade name"), 5. Put in a tender, 6. Trade secret, 7. Complaints, 8. Faulty goods, 9. Prospective customers, 10. Trade discount, 11. proposals, 12. Transactions.

**G. Receipts & Invoices:** 1A, 2C, 3B, 4a. GST 4b. VAT, 5. PST, 6. $33.66, 7. 15/02/--, 8. 18/02/--, 9. 10%, 10. Quantity.

# *Assorted business activity*

## 1. Agriculture & Forestry

**Make hay while the sun shines: 1.** People: Farmer – Landowner – Farm labourer – Farmhand – Farm Manager – Forest ranger – Woodcutter – Beekeeper – Vintner **2.** Working the land: Cereal – Poultry – Stock – Dairy – Organic – Market Gardening – Sea farming – A timber forest – A tea plantation - vineyard **3.** Farm machinery: Tractor – Combine Harvester – Trailer – Chain saw **4.** Farm buildings: Outbuildings – Farmyard – Silo – Shed – Barn – A lumber mill **5.** Farm Produce: Vegetables – Fruit – Crops – Mushrooms – Tropical crops **6:** Livestock: Cattle breeding – A flock of sheep – A litter of pigs – Thoroughbred horses **7:** Fieldwork for a bumper crop: Plow – Sow – Fertilize – Harvest **8:** Forest exploitation: Plant – Fell – Season – Market **9:** Problems which reduce crop yield: Pollution – Weeds – Rodents – Barren land – Drought – Bad crop rotation – Deforestation

## 2. Money & Banking

**A. A few financial antonyms:** 1. Borrow, 2. Deflation, 3. Mark-up, 4. Expenditure, 5. Bankrupt (or insolvent), 6. Withdraw, 7. In the black, 8. Loss, 9. Net, 10. Overcharged, 11. Spend, 12. Priceless

**B. A visit to Counting House Coffer Bank:** 1. Branch Manager, 2. Bank statement, 3. Current account, 4. Teller, 5. Savings account / Deposit account, 6. ATM (Automatic Teller Machine), 7. PIN, 8. Cheque / Check book, 9. Counterfoil / Stub, 10. Coins and notes, 11. Foreign currency, 12. Exchange rate, 13. Mortgage, 14. Loan, 15. Mortgage repayment, 16. Maturity date, 17. Home banking

**C. Umpteen confusing words:** 1. alone / lonely, 2. until / as far as, 3. audience / spectators, 4. Most / The most, 5. homework / housework, 6. valueless / invaluable, 7. game / play, 8. trip / travel / journey / voyage

**D. An investment on the stock market:** 1. INSIDER DEALING REVEALED 2. INVEST IN BLUE-CHIP COMPANIES 3. A BULL MARKET AT LAST 4. THE COMMODITY MARKET

**E. Acronyms:** APR: Annualized Percentage Rate, ASAP: As Soon As Possible, ATM: Automatic Teller Machine, BSI: British Standards Institute, CADM: Computer Assisted Design and Manufacturing, CEO: Chief Executive Officer, CPI: Consumer Price Index,

DDD: Deadline Delivery Date, ERP: Enterprise Requirement Planning, FAI: First Article Inspection, ERM: Exchange Rate Mechanism, FYI: For Your Information, NCV: No Commercial Value, PDCA: Plan, Do, Check, Act, POS: Point of sale, PTO: Please Turn Over, OEM: Original Equipment Manufacturer, VAT: Value Added Tax, SAE: Stamped Addressed Envelope, SKU: Stock Keeping Unit, WWW: World Wide Web, YTD: Year To Date, OTC: Over The Counter, ROI: Return On Investment, OTD: On Time Delivery, FAQ: Frequently Asked Questions

## 3. Insurance

**A. Have you got insurance coverage?** DIFFERENT KINDS OF INSURANCE: – Life assurance – Burglary insurance – Insure baggage against loss – Car insurance – Casualty insurance – Health insurance – Marine insurance – Life insurance – Annuity policy FULL COVERAGE: full coverage – all risks policy – Third-party fire and theft – Comprehensive TAKING OUT INSURANCE: Insurance policy – Certificate of insurance – Assess value – To be covered by insurance – To be insured PAYMENTS – YOU PAY: Annual Insurance premium – Annuity due – YOU GET: Annuity – settlement for the claim PUT IN A CLAIM: Damage – Injured party – Assess damage – Act of God – Act of vandalism – Fair wear and tear BEARING THE RISKS: underwriter – to underwrite

**B. Countless confusing words:** 1. borrow / lend, 2. spilt / pour, 3. priceless / worthless, 4. recipe / receipt, 5. good / right, 6. tell / say

## 4. Land Settlement & Zoning Regulations

**A. Urban planning & who is involved:** 1. Local authorities 2. Mayor (and deputy mayor) 3. Town council 4. Business Park 5. Business premises 6. Pedestrian precinct 7. Shopping district 8. Business development zone 9. Chartered Surveyor 10. Architect 11. Industrial Estate 12. Urban activity zone 13. Property Developer 14. Housing Estate

**B. Let's do some town planning:** 1.D, 2.F, 3.H, 4.C (or mass transit system), 5.A, 6.I, 7.E, 8.G, 9.B

## 5. Legal Matters

**A little bit of legal jargon:** 1.a, 2.b (An heir is someone who inherits) 3.b / c, 4.c, 5.b / c, 6.a, 7.a / b, 8.b, 9.b, 10.c, 11.a / c (A crook has been proven guilty), 12.a, 13.b, 14.c, 15.b / c, 16.a

## 6. The Media

**A. The Printed word:** 1. Circulation 2. Readership 3. Daily 4. Coverage 5. Features 6. Freelance 7. Editor 8. Headlines 9. Copyright 10. Complimentary copy 11. Subscription 12. Page rate 13. Renewal 14. Press Clipping 15. Newsletter 16. Proofreaders 17. Going to press 18. Printing works 19. Print run 20. Royalties

**B. Here we go again!** - homonyms: 1. patients / patience 2. weak / week 3. witch / which 4. wear / where 5. weather / whether 6. would / wood.

**C. Television & Radio:** Programs: Weather forecast – Quiz show – TV Cartoon – Commercial – Game show – Reality show – Chat / talk show – Sports Program – Variety show – Documentary – Current affairs program – Serial – Sitcom - Soap opera – Thriller – News – Equipment: Cable TV – Satellite TV – AM/FM Radio – Remote Control – DVD Player, Verbs: Turn on – Turn off – Turn over – Turn up – Turn down - Censor People: Newsreader – Broadcaster – Guest – Host – Viewer – Couch Potato, NB: Program (USA) Programme (UK): 1. Sports program 2. Commercials 3. Newsreader / news anchor 4. Quiz show / game show 5. Cable TV and satellite TV 6. Viewers 7. Turn off / turn over / change channel 8. Current affairs program

## 7. Real Estate & Corporate Property

**A. Accommodation:** 1. Detached / single family homes 2. Semi-detached 3. terraced / row houses (party wall) 4. Cottage 5. Bungalow 6. Caravan 7. Mobile home 8. Houseboat 9. Housing estate 10. Flat / apartment 11. Tower block 12. Office block 13. Turnkey factory 14. Flatlet / bedsit 15. Skyscraper

**B. Inside the house:** 1. Office / study 2. staircase 3. basement / cellar 4. kitchen 5. bathroom 6. bedroom 7. attic 8. garage 9. spare room / guest room 10. living / family / sitting room 11. hall / hallway 12. landing

**C. Renting property:** 1. Office space to let 2. Tenancy agreement 3. (To) rent 4. Life tenancy 5. To let 6. Sub-lease / sublet

**D. Purchasing property:** (1) estate agency (2) estate agent / realtor (3) particulars of sale (4) plot / patch (5) leasehold (6) freehold (7) restricted or unrestricted access (8) survey (9) provisional sales agreement (10) time-share property (11) ownership (12) gazumped (UK) (13) property deed (14) housewarming party

**E. A new landlord:** People: home owner, tenant, neighbour, surveyor, estate agent, landlord, landowner Moving house: housing allowance, decorate, relocate, removal

**F. The construction industry:** 1. surveyor (a person) 2. Design-build contract – "one-stop shopping" (you only need contact with one person) 3. General contractor (again, one person to do everything)

# Answer Section

4. Building site (the others are different types of construction) 5. Cost overrun (the others are construction materials) 6. Zoning and building requirements (the law, the others are building materials)

**G. Public Utilities:** 1.F, 2.T, 3.F, 4.F, 5.T, 6.T, 7.F, 8.T, 9.T, 10.T

### 8. Volunteer Work

**Charity begins at home :** 1. Financial gain 2. Humanitarian organisation 3. Needy areas 4. Local branch 5. Charity shop 6. Raise money 7. Rummage sales 8. Fund raiser 9. Sponsored marathon 10. Monthly donation

## *Communicating*

### 1. Letters, Faxes, E-mails

**A. A bit of letter writing:** 1.e, 2.s, 3.n, 4.k, 5.aa, 6.v, 7.r, 8.h, 9.cc, 10.u, 11.b, 12.l, 13.q, 14.o, 15.g, 16.y, 17.t, 18.a, 19.w, 20.j, 21.dd, 22.d, 23.x, 24.z, 25.m, 26.c, 27.bb, 28.i, 29.p, 30.f

**B. What's in a name?:** Full name: James Adam Smith, Surname: Smith, First name: James, Middle name: Adam, Nickname: Jimbo

**C. Get the title right:** 1.B, 2.D, 3.A, 4.C

**D. Sending an e-mail:** @ = at; . = dot; company = com; send on = forward; United Kingdom = uk; organisation = org; erase = delete; unsolicited message = spam

**E. Where does it go?:**

| | | |
|---|---|---|
| 8 | | 5 |
| | 1 | |
| 3 | 7 | 4 |
| 6 | 2 | |

### 2. Telephone

**A. Thank you for calling:** 1 D, 2 K, 3 F, 4 I, 5 N, 6 A, 7 G, 8 C, 9 J, 10 L, 11 B, 12 H, 13 M, 14 E

**B. Is he on the blower?** 1.b, 2.b, 3.a, 4.a, 5.b, 6.a, 7.b, 8.b, 9.b, 10.a, 11.b, 12.a, 13.a, 14.b, 15.b, 16.a

### 3. Contracts

**A. Lay down the regulations:** 1. retainer 2. to comply with 3. small print 4. by right 5. confirmed in writing 6. set forth 7. dotted line 8. liable 9. bona fide 10. is binding 11. undersigned 12. subject to 13. read and approved 14. unless otherwise stipulated 15. abide by 16. unwritten agreement 17. price in effect 18. antedated 19. undertake 20. in triplicate

**B. Understanding the agreement:** 1.G, 2.I, 3.E, 4.B, 5.J, 6.D, 7.A, 8.F, 9.C, 10.H

**C. The beginning, the middle and the end:** 1. Commencing 2. Term of notice 3. Rider 4. Affidavit 5. Waiver 6. Breach of contract 7. Completion date 8. Terminate

**D. Compound nouns:** 1. minerals (no "s"– the first word in a compound is like an adjective) 2. Travelling (no "–ing") 3. Money (turnover can be financial but not money) 4. Myself (not a reflexive pronoun) 5. Coffee (which is served in a cup or mug, not a glass) 6. Peanut (you eat peanut butter) 7. Cell phone – no "'s" for possession 8. Greeting – for once there should be an "s" as there are more than one greeting = greetings 9. Tickets (no "s") 10. Parenting = parental 11. Interests (no "s") 12. Ware – It's shareware (the share describes the kind of ware it is and is the "adjective" part of the compound) 13. bathing – it's a bathroom! 14. "Pink" wine is called rosé in English too. 15. five-minutes (no "s").

### 4. Meetings & Appointments

**A. Let me look in my diary:** 1. $1^{st}$, 2. $31^{st}$ May, 3. $4^{th}$ & $5^{th}$, 4. $13^{th}$, 5. $11^{th}$ & $12^{th}$, 6. $18^{th}$ & $19^{th}$, 7. $8^{th}$ – $10^{th}$, 8. $14^{th}$ & $28^{th}$, 9. $17^{th}$ – $24^{th}$, 10. $6^{th}$ & $7^{th}$, 11. $30^{th}$ June, $1^{st}$ July, 12. $15^{th}$ – $17^{th}$, 13. $4^{th}$ & $5^{th}$ July, 14. $29^{th}$

**B. Sunrise or sunset?:** 1.E, 2.P, 3.K, 4.T, 5.O, 6.B, 7.L (or two thousand and twelve), 8.I, 9.R, 10.N, 11.G, 12.A, 13.J, 14.D, 15.Q, 16.S, 17.C, 18.H, 19.M, 20.F

**C. The meeting has been deferred:** Organise the meeting for 18th March, 2009 = arrange / fix / set up: Watch out! Meeting in 7 days' time! = give a week's warning: 12th June, 2010, to 6th July, 2010 = Defer / postpone / put back: 9th November, 2009, to 30th October, 2009 = Bring forward: 8th January, 2009, to never! = Cancel / be off

**D. Kinds of meeting:** 1. Quarterly, 2. Steering committee, 3. AGM (Annual General Meeting), 4. Board (of Directors), 5. Briefing / debriefing, 6. Study group, 7. Think tank, 8. Task Force, 9. Committee, 10. seminar

**E. Organisation:** 1. available 2. suitable 3. notify 4. agenda 5. chair (i.e. run the meeting) / be chairperson 6. limit 7. minutes of meeting 8. proxy vote 9. any other business 10. sum up 11. record (of the meeting) 12. report 13. task, 14. conference call.

**F. A few useful expressions:** 1 E, 2 H, 3 M, 4 J, 5 B, 6 L, 7 K, 8 I, 9 F, 10 D, 11 N, 12 G, 13 C, 14 A

## 5. Negotiating

**A. A bit of bargaining:** A: 11.2.17., B: 5.20.7., C: 19. 13.16., D: 4.9.18., E: 21.12.6., F: 10.1.15., G: 3.14.8.
**B. 6 more confusing words:** 1. sensible / sensitive 2. shade / shadow 3. talk / speaks 4. teach / learn 5. wander / wonder 6. Look at / watches
**C. I just had a thought:** 1.D, 2.F, 3.B, 4.J, 5.G, 6.I, 7.A, 8.E, 9.H, 10.C

## 6. Presentations & Graphs

**A. Equipment for a presentation:** 1. Handout 2. Screen 3. Slides 4. Flipchart 5. (Laser) pointer 6. Whiteboard 7. Data projector / beamer 8. Overhead projector (OHP)
**B. What kind of graph shall I use?:** 1. Run chart / line graph 2. Pie Chart 3. Bar Chart 4. Organisation Chart 5. Flowchart 6. Cause and effect diagram (A diagram can show how something works, interaction between different variables...) 7. Spreadsheet 8. Value Stream Mapping
**C. Ups & downs:** Go up / improve: 1, 7, 12 Go down / deteriorate: 2, 5, 10, 11 Even out / remain stable: 3, 8, 9 Top and bottom: 4, 6

## 7. Small Talk

**A. A little social chit-chat:** 1. Have a good trip / journey. 2. How do you do? I'm pleased to meet you. 3. Shall we / let's break for lunch. That's a good idea. 4. Would you like a cup of coffee? 5. How are you? It's nice to see you again. 6. I'm afraid / I'm sorry, but he will be late. 7. I have an appointment / a meeting with Mr. Smith. 8. See you later / on Friday. 9. How's the company / business? 10. Welcome to Birmingham Mr. / Mrs. / Miss / Ms. Smith / Peter. 11. I do not agree = I think it's a bad idea. 12. What's your line of business? / What business are you in? 13. What's your full name? Joan Smith. 14. Could we fix / arrange an appointment? 15. I do appreciate you coming so early. 16. Does that suit you? / Is that convenient?
**B. What wonderful weather:** 1.C, 2.J, 3.G, 4.O, 5.L, 6.B, 7.N, 8.F, 9.M, 10.I, 11.A, 12.K, 13.P, 14.D, 15.H, 16.E
**C. What's the temperature?:** Below freezing – Freezing cold – Chilly – Cool – Mild – Warm – Hot – Boiling hot
**D. Colourful expressions:**

| Black | Black & blue | Black & white | Brown | Blue | Grey |
|---|---|---|---|---|---|
| 1, 20 | 5 | 9 | 8 | 4, 15, 16 | 11, 14 |

| Green | Pink | Red | White | Yellow | Rainbow |
|---|---|---|---|---|---|
| 2, 10 | 7, 17 | 3, 12, 18 | 19 | 13 | 6 |

# *Travelling & entertainment*

## 1. Travelling

**A. Globe-trotting:** 1.B, 2.D, 3.A, 4.E, 5.C
**B. A touch of ecotourism:** 1. Package deal 2. Vacation (Holiday in UK English) 3. Affordable 4. All-inclusive 5. Off-season 6. Peak-season 7. Accommodation 8. Vacancies 9. Transfers 10. Valid passport 11. Traveler's check (Traveller's cheque in UK English) 12. Departure date.
**C. Flying out:** 1.K, 2.P, 3.T, 4.Y, 5.B, 6.S, 7.V, 8.X, 9.M, 10.I, 11.A, 12.U, 13.R, 14.J, 15.F, 16.C, 17.Z, 18.E, 19.L, 20.N, 21.W, 22.D, 23.H, 24.O, 25.Q, 26. G
**D. Problems and yet more problems:** 1. Overweight 2. Delayed 3. Cancelled 4. Overbooked 5. Customs regulations 6. Invalid 7. Steward 8. Rerouted
**E. On the road again:** 1. 8. 13. 16. 3. 10. 7. 14. 18. 4. 20. 9. 15. 2. 19. 11. 5. 17. 12. 6.
**F. Car hire or rental:** Mini – economy – compact – intermediate – standard – full-size – premium – luxury – convertible – sports car – limousine – minivan – full-size van – pick-up truck – sport utility vehicle (SUV) – station wagon : 1.D (tick), 2.F (tick), 3.J, 4.I, 5.B (tick), 6.E, 7.H, 8.A, 9.C, 10.G (tick)
**G. Taking a taxi (or cab):** 1.F, 2.T, 3.T (Usually marked inside the taxi), 4.F, 5.T, 6.T, 7.T, 8.F (about €90), 9.T, 10.F, 11.F, 12.T, 13.T, 14.F (about 10%)
**H. So the train takes the strain:** 1.D, 2.M, 3.J, 4.S, 5.G, 6.Q, 7.B, 8.O, 9.K, 10.I, 11.E, 12.T, 13.A, 14.P, 15.R, 16.N, 17.F, 18.C, 19.L, 20.H
NB: Subway (USA) Underground / tube (UK) Metro (Paris)
**I. On the bus:** 1. Fares 2. Crowded 3. Bus stop 4. Through bus (Express) 5. Bus service 6. Double Decker 7. Season ticket 8. Missed
**J. We took the ferry:** Ferry – hovercraft – foot passengers – boarding lounge – crossing – ship – calm – rough
**K. Homonyms for hopping around:** 1. aisle / isle 2. aloud / allowed 3. find / fined 4. for / four 5. sail / sale 6. through / threw
**L. Booking Hotel Accommodation:** 1. inclusive, 2. half-board, 3. rates, 4. Check in / sign in, 5. check out / sign out, 6. facilities
**M. Choose your hotel room:** Double – 1 bed for 2 people; En-suite – with private bathroom; Single – for 1 person; Suite – with bedroom and sitting room; Twin – 2 single beds; Family – for parents and children
**N. What kind of accommodation?:** A. Youth hostel

B. Holiday cottage C. In the capital, luxury hotel, all-inclusive D. Motel in a nearby suburb E. B&B in the countryside F. Full board G. Budget hotel in the outskirts of the city H. Apartment hotel, half board I. Condo hotel J. Self-catering

**O. Customary complaints:** 1.D, 2.J, 3.G, 4.M, 5.B, 6K, 7.F, 8.N, 9.H, 10.L, 11.A, 12.O, 13.C, 14.I, 15.P, 16.E, NB: Elevator (USA) Lift (UK) Bellhop (USA) Bellboy (UK)

**P. Laundry & dry cleaning:** OUTDOOR WEAR: G&L: raincoat, overcoat, hat BUSINESS WEAR: G&L: suit (jacket and trousers / jacket and skirt), shirt, G: tie, L: dress, skirt, blouse CASUAL WEAR: G&L: trousers, jeans, sweater / pullover, shirt, cardigan SPORTS WEAR: G&L: tracksuit, t-shirt, sweatshirt, NIGHT WEAR: G: pyjamas, L: nightdress, G&L: dressing gown UNDERWEAR: G&L: socks, pants (underpants), vest (undershirt) L: bra, stockings, tights

## 2. Health Care

**A. Know your body:** 1. Head, 2. Hair, 3. Eye, 4. Nose, 5. Mouth, 6. Chin, 7. Throat, 8. Chest, 9. Arm, 10. Back, 11. Wrist, 12. Hand, 13. Leg, 14. Foot, 15. Heel, 16. Toe, 17. Ankle, 18. Knee, 19. Finger, 20. Thumb, 21. Hip, 22. Elbow, 23. Stomach, 24. Shoulder, 25. Neck, 26. Tooth (2 teeth), 27. Ear, 28. Eyebrow

**B. So what's the matter with you?:** 1. Senior Citizen & G.P. (General practitioner) – doctor's surgery 2. Student & doctor – doctor's surgery 3. Housewife & psychologist – psychologist's office 4. Star or model & plastic surgeon - luxurious clinic 5. Elderly person & dentist – dentist's surgery 6. Patient waiting for surgery & anaesthetist – hospital 7. Man going deaf & ENT specialist – in his successful practice 8. Short-sighted person and eye specialist – eye clinic.

**C. What treatment do you need?** 1.D, 2.G, 3.J, 4.F, 5.I, 6.A, 7.H, 8.C, 9.E, 10.B

**D. Have you got medical insurance?:** 1.Private 2. Welfare 3. Complementary 4. Premium 5. Alternative 6. Disability 7. Screening 8. Referrals 9. Nursing 10. Prescription 11. Hearing 12. Deductibles

## 3. Wining & Dining

**A. Eating out:** PLACES TO EAT: cafeteria – restaurant – wine bar – eatery – pizza house – tea room – drive-in / WHO YOU MIGHT SEE: waiter – waitress – waiting staff - chef - wine waiter - bartender / VARIOUS KINDS OF MEAL: business lunch – family dinner – a snack with mates – nibbles with drinks – drinks at happy hour / THE STAGES IN A MEAL: starter – main course – dessert – cheese – doggie bag / EQUIPMENT FOR MEALTIME: booster seat – napkin – tablecloth – highchair – booth – cutlery – crockery – glassware / DIFFERENT WAYS OF COOKING: fry – boil – roast – smoke – grill – bake – steam – poach

**B. Let's go out for a meal:** A: 1. 5. 2. 4. 3. / B: 1. 7. 4. 2. 6. 3. 8. 5. / C: 1. 9. 3. 8. 14. 6. 12. 10. 4. 13. 7. 11. 5. 2. / D: 1. 8. 5. 9. 2. 6. 10. 3. 7. 4. / E: 1. 5. 8. 2. 6. 9. 3. 7. 4.

**C. What's in the refrigerator?:** MEAT: beef – lamb – pork – mutton – veal / POULTRY: egg – goose – chicken – guinea fowl – turkey – frogs' legs – duck / VEGETABLES & SALAD: cauliflower – brussels sprouts – beans – turnip – leeks – asparagus – green / red pepper – mushrooms – carrots – peas – potatoes – cabbage – spinach – tomato - lettuce – cucumber – avocado pear / FISH & SEAFOOD: oysters – trout – shrimp – scallops - kipper – mussels – prawns – pike – salmon – lobster GAME: Pheasant – hare – partridge – wild boar – venison – rabbit / DESSERT / PUDDING & FRUIT: pineapple – lemon – banana – raspberry – pancake – apple – fruit salad – grapefruit – blackcurrant – pear – grapes – ice cream – lime – custard – orange

**D. Arranging a wedding banquet:** 1.C 2.E 3.G 4.I 5.A 6.H 7.F 8.B 9.J 10.D

## 4. Leisure & The Arts

**A. At the 5-screen cinema:** 1. Blockbuster 2. Trailer 3. Screening time 4. Director 5. Drive-in movie 6. Release 7. Actor 8. Box Office 9. Low-Budget Film 10. Soundtrack 11. Award 12. Flop 13. Movie theatre 14. Scenery

**B. A full-length film or short feature:** 1. Silent movie 2. Drama 3. Science Fiction 4. Western 5. Horror 6. Action 7. Musical 8. Adventure 9. Comedy 10. Historical 11. Cartoon 12. War

**C. Theatre & shows:** 1. F 2.F 3.T 4.F 5.T 6.T 7.F 8.F

**D. Exhibitions and museums:** 1.a 2.b 3.b 4.a 5.a 6.b 7.a 8.b 9.a 10.a 11.b 12.a

**E. Fictional and non-fictional literature:** short-story, autobiography, essays, poetry, journal, prose, novel, myth, diary, folktale, biography

**F. A good read:** 1.-, 2.-, 3.+, 4.-, 5.-, 6. +, 7.-, 8.-, 9. +, 10.-, 11. +, 12. +

**G. Can you play music by ear?:** 1) concert 2) orchestra 3) conductor 4) musicians 5) choir 6) classical 7) latecomers 8) jazz 9) festival 10) amateur

**H. Fame at last:** 1.C, 2.E, 3.A, 4.D, 5.F, 6.B

**I. At the match:** 1.C, 2.A, 3.B, 4.E, 5.D, 6.H, 7.F, 8.I, 9.G, 10.K, 11.J, 12.O, 13.L, 14.M, 15.N (Can also be a noun – a score)

**J. A trip to the zoo with the family:** 1. twin 2. great uncle's 3. grandmother and grandfather 4. step-mother (step-daughter / father / brother 5. half brother (sister) 6. grandchildren (granddaughter / grandson 7. niece and nephew 8. father in-law (mother / sister / brother-in-law) NB: B2W & ATB = Back to work and all the best

**K. One word, many meanings:** 1. Quote, 2. Issue, 3. meet, 4. plant, 5. tip, 6. launch, 7. miss

**L. High Days and Holidays:** 1. No 2. Yes – the day is replaced by a working day but not necessarily the same one (see Christmas!) 3. No – USA 10 / UK 8 4. USA – Yes (4th July) / UK – No 5. Yes – New Year's Day, Christmas Day 6. No 7. Yes – Veteran's Day, Thankgiving Day, Saint Patrick's Day, Easter Tuesday, Orangeman's Day 8. No

**Just a warm-up:** 1. I must call the supplier this afternoon. 2. I agree 3. What is Mary like? She is attractive and bright. 4. How long does it take you to go to work? 5. He was much fatter 10 years ago 6. I look forward to hearing from you. Yours faithfully..... 7. She is responsible for (in charge of) quality 8. The economic situation is not very good. 9. He works all day every day of the week. 10. We are interested in your proposal. 11. I want you to pay attention. 12. Firstly / first, we'll look at the pie chart. 13. I would like some information about.... 14. It's high time you spoke fluent English! 15. You mustn't touch that handle! 16. One of the managers has forgotten their laptop. 17. There are people who have no ambition. 18. I'd rather you used the other phone. 19. Never have I seen such an efficient production line. 20. Nowhere are people so hardworking as in our company, there is such a lot to do!

FSC
www.fsc.org
MIXTE
Papier issu de sources responsables
FSC® C022030

Achevé d'imprimer en avril 2017
sur les presses de la Nouvelle Imprimerie Laballery
58500 Clamecy
Dépôt légal : mai 2017
Numéro d'impression : 704208
N° d'éditeur : 10213147 - ALINEA
*Imprimé en France*

La Nouvelle Imprimerie Laballery est titulaire de la marque Imprim'Vert®